Insight Bible Commentary Series

The Book of Mark

Volume I: Chapters 1-6

Randy Lariscy

WordTruth Press℠
USA

Copyright © 2013, Randy Lariscy

All rights reserved.

1st Edition published by WordTruth Press℠ in the United States (SAN: 920-2811). Find us on the web at WordTruthPress.com. You can contact WordTruth Press by phone at 404.919.WORD (9673) or by email at Info@WordTruthPress.com.

Scripture taken from the Holy Bible, NEW INTERNATIONAL VERSION®. Copyright © 1973, 1978, 1984, 2011 by Biblica, Inc. All rights reserved worldwide. Used by permission.

NEW INTERNATIONAL VERSION® and NIV® are registered trademarks of Biblica, Inc. Use of either trademark for the offering of goods or services requires the prior written consent of Biblica US, Inc.

Scripture noted as NKJV taken from the New King James Version®. Copyright © 1982 by Thomas Nelson, Inc. Used by permission. All rights reserved.

Library of Congress Control Number: 2012950522

ISBN-13: 978-0-9852899-3-5

Acknowledgements

As a genre, Bible commentaries are generally dry reading. One exception to this rule is the commentary from Thru the Bible Radio by the late Dr. J. Vernon McGee. Written in plain, matter of fact fashion, Dr. McGee's work brought the Scriptures to life for me along with millions of others. The Insight Bible Commentary series is dedicated to the memory of one of the world's great Bible teachers. I never met him on Earth but look forward to the day when I can greet him in Heaven.

 **Insight Bible Commentary Series**

Contents

I. Overview of the Gospel of Mark 15
    A. Purpose of Mark's Gospel. 15
        (1) The priority of purpose over content. 15
        (2) Finding the purpose in Mark's Gospel. 16
        (3) The significance of the gospel. 17
        (4) The amazing truth about Jesus. 18
        (5) The focus of Mark's account. 21
        (6) The key verse. 22
    B. Authorship of Mark's Gospel. 24
        (1) Who wrote the gospel? 24
        (2) What do we know about Mark? 26
        (3) When was the gospel written? 27
        (4) What is the manuscript evidence for the gospel of Mark? 29
    C. Outline and Chronology of Mark's Gospel. 29
    D. Contribution of Mark's Gospel 32

II. Jesus Prepares For His Earthly Ministry (Mark 1:2-13). 35
    A. Jesus is announced by John the Baptist (Mark 1:2-8). 35

 Insight Bible Commentary Series

    B. Jesus is identified by God as His beloved Son (Mark 1:9-11). 48

    C. Jesus overcomes temptation in the wilderness (Mark 1:12-13). 55

    D. Conclusion of Section 2. 58

III. Jesus Begins His Earthly Ministry in Galilee (Mark 1:14-3:35) 61

    A. In Capernaum (Mark 1:14-34). 61

        (1) Jesus proclaims the message of His ministry (Mark 1:14-15). 61

        (2) Jesus calls His first disciples (Mark 1:16-20). 68

        (3) Jesus commands authority over demons (Mark 1:21-28). 73

        (4) Jesus commands power over sickness (Mark 1:29-31). 85

        (5) Jesus commands power over all who are sick (Mark 1:32-34). 87

    B. Traveling Through Galilee (Mark 1:35-2:12). 91

        (1) Jesus proclaims the purpose of His ministry (Mark 1:35-39). 91

        (2) Jesus heals a leper (Mark 1:40-45) 95

        (3) Jesus forgives the sins of a lame man (Mark 2:1-12). 104

    C. Encountering Questions (Mark 2:13-3:6). 123

        (1) Jesus ministers to publicans and sinners (Mark 2:13-17). 123

(2) Jesus delineates new ways for the new life He offers (Mark 2:18-22). 133

(3) Jesus defies the Sabbath traditions of men (Mark 2:23-28). 137

(4) Pharisees begin their plot to kill Jesus (Mark 3:1-6).. 141

D. Organizing the Disciples (Mark 3:7-35). 145

(1) Jesus teaches multitudes from Israel and the surrounding nations. (Mark 3:7-12). 145

(2) Jesus calls out His twelve disciples (Mark 3:13-19).. 147

(3) Scribes accuse Jesus of being demon-possessed. (Mark 3:20-30). 150

(4) Jesus shares a close relationship with those who do God's will (Mark 3:31-35). 155

IV. Jesus Prepares His Disciples (Mark 4:1-6:6) 159

A. Jesus teaches His disciples through parables (Mark 4:1-34). 159

(1) Parable of the sower (Mark 4:1-9). 159

(2) Jesus explains His use of parables (Mark 4:10-12).... 162

(3) Jesus explains the parable of the Sower (Mark 4:13-20). 165

(4) Jesus announces the keys to understanding the Kingdom of God (Mark 4:21-25). 170

(5) Parable of the growing seed (Mark 4:26-29). 172

(6) Parable of the mustard seed (Mark 4:30-32). 173

(7) Jesus uses parables for the people but explains all to His disciples (Mark 4:33-34). 174

    B. Jesus teaches His disciples through miracles (Mark 4:35-6:6) 176

        (1) Jesus calms the wind and the sea (Mark 4:35-41) 176

        (2) Jesus drives out a legion of demons into a herd of pigs (Mark 5:1-20). 178

        (3) Jesus heals the sick and raises the dead (Mark 5:21-43). 183

        (4) Jesus heals only a few sick people in His hometown (Mark 6:1-6a). 193

V. Jesus Extends His Ministry Through His Disciples (Mark 6:6b-6:56) 201

    A. Jesus sends out the twelve to preach, heal, and cast out demons (Mark 6:6b-13). 201

    B. King Herod fears the power of John the Baptist in Jesus (Mark 6:14-29). 205

    C. Jesus feeds five thousand with five loaves of bread and two fish (Mark 6:30-44). 215

    D. Jesus walks on water (Mark 6:45-52). 221

    E. Jesus heals all that touch Him in the land of Gennesaret (Mark 6:53-56) 226

Complete Outline of Mark 231
About the Author 243

The Book of Mark (Volume One)

Insight Bible Commentary Series

I. Overview of the Gospel of Mark

The beginning of the good news about Jesus the Messiah, the Son of God. (Mark 1:1, NIV®)

No commentary on the Bible can begin without a proper context. The Insight Bible Commentary on the Gospel of Mark will establish this context in the following sections:

A. Purpose

B. Authorship

C. Outline and Chronology

D. Contribution

The intent of this commentary is to provide insights into God's word that will not only help you understand the meaning of Scripture but apply it in your own life in meaningful ways.

A. Purpose of Mark's Gospel.

(1) The priority of purpose over content.

Anytime a writer attempts to put pen to paper, that writer must have a clear purpose in writing. Without a clear purpose, the resulting prose will be disorganized, incoherent, and

 Insight Bible Commentary Series

unreadable. However, with a clear purpose in mind, the writer can focus the story or account using the most important points to accomplish the purpose. Likewise, in order to understand any written work, you must somehow ascertain the purpose of the writer. Without understanding the purpose, you can read into a written work a meaning that was never intended by the writer. For instance, if you read poetry, you are not expected to take the figures of speech or exaggerations literally. If you did, you would misunderstand the meaning intended by the writer. On the other hand, if you read an historical work, you would not want to take the facts presented as allegories or figures of speech. To do so would also confuse the meaning intended by the writer. The purpose of a written work guides both the writing and the reading of it.

(2) Finding the purpose in Mark's Gospel.

In many books, you find a preface written by the author explaining exactly why and on what occasion the book was written. The Bible is a collection of sixty-six books, some of which have the purpose explicitly stated, such as the gospel of John which reads:

> *³⁰ Jesus performed many other signs in the presence of his disciples, which are not recorded in this book. ³¹ But these are written that you may believe that Jesus is the Messiah, the Son of God, and that by believing you may have life in his name. (John 20:30-31, NIV®)*

So the purpose of the gospel of John is to unfold specific events in the life of Jesus so that you will understand and believe that Jesus is the Christ.

The gospel of Mark presents the purpose of its writing in the very first verse:

> *The beginning of the good news about Jesus the Messiah, the Son of God. (Mark 1:1, NIV®)*

What is the purpose of the book of Mark? The purpose is to show how the good news of Jesus Christ began and why His followers claim that He is the Son of God.

(3) The significance of the gospel.

What Mark begins in this account of the life of Jesus Christ is "*good news*" from the Greek *euaggelion*. Mark had good news to share. The coming of Jesus Christ into the world meant the fulfillment of God's promise to mankind that He would deal once and for all with the problem of sin (Gen. 3:15).

People would no longer be separated from God because of their sin but, through Jesus Christ, could be forgiven and reconciled to God. God provided a way for people to have forgiveness and eternal life through His Son, Jesus Christ (John 14:6; Rom. 5:8; 1 John 5:11-13). This is good news indeed!

(4) The amazing truth about Jesus.

Mark begins this account of the life of Jesus Christ with a straightforward declaration: Jesus is the Son of God. Introductions are important in how you relate to a person. Mark introduces us to a divine revelation about Jesus: He is the Christ, the Son of God. In the first chapter of Mark, Jesus is introduced as both a human being and as the Son of God. Jesus was fully human and fully divine. Jesus is God in human form.

The title "*Son of ...*" (Mark 1:1, NIV®) can refer to the physical child of a man and woman, or a descendent of a family line. The Bible uses the phrase this way in over 1,100 verses. Does this mean that God has a wife somewhere and through His wife He conceived a Son? While this sounds like a crazy premise, it is actually taught by the Mormons as well as other equally confused theological cults. The answer to this question is definitively "No." The Bible tells us that God is spirit in nature: *"God is spirit, and his worshipers must worship in the Spirit and in truth."* (John 4:24, NIV®) Note that God is not "a Spirit" in the sense of being localized, in only one place at one time. God IS spirit in nature, infinite spirit, without beginning and without end. As a spiritual being, God does not have a physical body that conceives children.

So what does the phrase *"the Son of God"* (Mark 1:1, NIV®) really mean? In the time the Bible was written, one was also called a "son of" something to describe what that person was like. Elisha called the king of Israel the *"son of a murderer"* (2 Kings 6:32, NKJV)[1] because of his murderous intent toward the prophet of God. The Psalmist called the enemies of God the *"son of wickedness"* (Psalm 89:22, NKJV). Isaiah satirized the princes of Zoan who thought of themselves as *"son of the wise, The son of ancient kings"* (Isaiah 19:11, NKJV). Here the reference is the characteristic of wisdom and royal ancestry. Daniel used the phrase *"Son of God"* (Daniel 3:25, NKJV) as the king described the heavenly figure (most likely the preincarnate Christ) in the furnace with Shadrach, Meshach, and Abednego. Daniel also describes a vision of Christ as the *"Son of Man"*

---

[1] *The NIV® refers simply to "murderer." The Greek text is* ben-ratsach *which means son of a murderer.*

(Daniel 7:13, NKJV) because of His appearance in human form. Jesus used the phrase *"son of peace"* (Luke 10:6, NKJV) to refer to a peaceful welcome. Judas, who betrayed Jesus, was called the *"son of perdition"* (John 17:12; 2 Thessalonians 2:3, NKJV). Barnabas was called the *"Son of Encouragement"* (Acts 4:36, NIV®) because he was a great encourager of his brothers and sisters in Christ. And we should encourage one another just as Barnabas did.

Calling Jesus the *"Son of God"* (1:1, NIV®) means that He has the character of God. It also means that Jesus shares the same divine nature as God. We find this same truth about Jesus in John 1:1, Acts 7:59, Acts 20:28, Philippians 2:6, Titus 3:4 and many other verses in the New Testament.

Some people look at Jesus as a great teacher. Some people see Him as a great prophet. Many see Jesus as just a man who lived a long time ago. None of these judgments are correct. In fact, to believe in a Jesus that is anything less than the Son of God is to believe in a different Jesus:

- Jesus who is not the Son of God cannot save you from your sins nor get you to Heaven (John 5:24).
- Jesus who is not the Son of God cannot be trusted to provide for your needs (Matthew 6:33).

- Jesus who is not the Son of God cannot be with you at all times, as He promised (Matthew 28:20).

This is why Mark reveals to us in the very first verse the vital truth about Jesus: He is the Son of God. Jesus has the character and nature of God. The Apostles were eye-witnesses of Jesus Christ before and after His resurrection. Except for the Apostle John, each of the apostles was murdered for his testimony that Jesus Christ is the Son of God. They could have denied that Jesus was the Son of God and lived. But they knew the truth and declared the truth about Jesus to the very end. And so should you and I as His disciples today.

(5) The focus of Mark's account.

When you read the gospel of Mark, you quickly see the focus is on the work of Jesus Christ. Personal details about Jesus' life are kept to a minimum. You do not find a lengthy explanation of Jesus' birth. You do not read a detailed chronology of His family. You do not know what town was Jesus' home. There are only a few teaching discourses in Mark's gospel. The bulk of the gospel is an account of the work Jesus performed. Clearly, Mark was trying to explain Jesus by what He did more than what He said.

In presenting this account of the life of Jesus, Mark reveals Jesus as the mighty Servant of God, always about the Father's business. The Greek word *eutheos*, translated *"immediately," "at once,"* and *"as soon as,"* is used forty times in just sixteen chapters. In fact, it is used nine times in just the first chapter. Mark uses this word not only to create dramatic tension in the story but to emphasize the nature of Jesus' earthly ministry. It was persistent and urgent in its motivation, active and constructive in its mission, purposeful in its result.

(6) The key verse.

Without question, the key verse in the gospel of Mark is found near the end of chapter ten:

> *For even the Son of Man did not come to be served, but to serve, and to give his life as a ransom for many. (Mark 10:45, NIV®)*

The measure of greatness, according to our LORD Jesus, is not the power and influence you exercise over others nor the wealth you accumulate nor the beauty you possess nor the talents you possess. The real measure of greatness is service. Jesus taught the disciples about true greatness in word and then modeled greatness for them in His life. *"This is how we know what love is: Jesus Christ laid down his life for us. And we ought to lay down our lives for our brothers and sisters."* (1 John 3:16, NIV®)

The gospel of Mark portrays Jesus on the move as the mighty Servant of God. The power of His might was in His selfless urgent service to others. The gospel characterizes Jesus' urgent work as:

- *"Immediately"* (Mark 2:8, 6:45, 10:52)
- *"At Once"* (Mark 1:12,43, 5:30)
- *"Just as"* (Mark 1:10, 14:43)
- *"As soon as"* (Mark 1:29, 6:54)

Jesus emphatically went here and there preaching the gospel and performing mighty signs and wonders to confirm the truth of His word. When Jesus entered a place or acted to heal and drive out demons (Mark 1:18,31,42, 2:2,12, 3:6, 4:5,15,16,17,29, 5:2,29,42, 6:25,54, 7:35, 9:15,20,24, 10:52, 11:3, 14:43,45, 15:1) things changed instantly. In the ultimate act of sacrificial service, Jesus willingly laid down His life for all mankind. The gospel of Mark was most likely written to a Roman audience. To the Romans, the death of this mighty Servant of God on the cross would be an unthinkable shame. As the key verse in the gospel, Mark 10:45 explains the reason for this extraordinary sacrifice. Jesus was mighty in deed and in

love. What appeared to be a shame was in reality a purposeful act of redemption. The resurrection of Christ confirmed the absolute victory and vindication of Christ in this ultimate act of sacrificial service.

B. Authorship of Mark's Gospel.

The beginning of the good news .... (Mark 1:1, NIV®)

(1) Who wrote the gospel?

The Gospel of Mark itself does not state its author. An ancient title *Kata Markon* at the beginning of the book translates as *"According to Mark."*[2] The early church fathers were unanimous that Mark wrote the gospel attributed to him, and that he wrote it in Rome. While they do not agree on when Mark wrote the gospel, they record that Mark wrote under the preaching and teaching of the Apostle Peter. The earliest reference to Mark's authorship is found in Papias, Bishop of

---

[2] Butler, Trent C. *Holman Bible Dictionary.* Nashville, Tennessee: Holman Bible Publishers. Copyright 1991. p. 920.

Hierapolis (ca. A.D. 140), who wrote in a book the following comment that was later quoted by Eusebius:

> *And the elder said this also: "Mark, having become the interpreter of Peter, wrote down accurately whatever he remembered of the things said and done by the Lord, but not however in order." For neither did he hear the Lord, nor did he follow him, but afterwards, as I said, Peter, who adapted his teachings to the needs of his hearers, but not as though he were drawing up a connected account of the Lord's oracles. So then Mark made no mistake in thus recording some things just as he remembered them. For he took forethought for one thing, not to omit any of the things that he had heard nor to state any of them falsely.*[3]

The next reference to Mark as the author comes from *"Justin Martyr (ca. A.D. 155)"* who *"mentioned the Memoirs of Peter that contained the words 'named Boanerges, which means "sons of thunder."'"*[4] This nickname for the two brothers, James and John, is found only in Mark's gospel (3:17). Both the Anti-Marcionite Prologue to the Gospels (ca. A.D. 160) and a later church father, Irenaeus (ca. A.D. 175), attribute the gospel to

---

[3] Lane, William L. *The New International Commentary on the New Testament: The Gospel of Mark.* Grand Rapids, Michigan: William B. Eerdmans Publishing Company. Copyright 1974. p. 8.
4 Brooks, James A. *The New American Commentary: Mark.* Nashville, Tennessee: Broadman Press. Copyright 1991. p. 18.

 Insight Bible Commentary Series

Mark.[5] It is worthy to note that in the Muratorian Canon, a church document listing books recognized as authoritative Scripture, the gospel of Mark was included (ca. A.D. 170). Mark is said to have been present at the preaching of Peter and so he recorded what he heard from the apostle.[6]

(2) What do we know about Mark?

As a young man, John Mark lived with his mother in Jerusalem (Acts 12:12). Mark's mother, Mary, had a house large enough to house the disciples for prayer meetings. The Apostle Peter met there with the disciples on a regular basis since he was well known to the servants (Acts 12:13-14). It could be that Mark and his family were led to faith in Christ by Peter (possible reference in 1 Peter 5:13, though Mark was a common Roman name). In any event, John Mark was chosen by Barnabas, his relative (Col. 4:10) and Saul to accompany them on their journey to Antioch and in their first evangelistic missions trip (Acts 12:25). At Pamphylia, John Mark apparently became afraid of the opposition and fled the missions party (Acts 13:13, ref. 15:38). Paul did not want to continue with John Mark but Barnabas was adamant that he be included. The conflict actually caused Barnabas and Paul to split up (Acts 15:39). Paul took

---
[5] *Lane. p. 9.*
[6] *Ibid. p. 9.*

Silas and headed to Syria and Cilicia (Acts 15:40-41). Barnabas took Mark with him to Cyprus (Acts 15:39). Near the end of Paul's life, we see that Mark had redeemed himself in Paul's eyes for Paul wrote to Timothy: *"Only Luke is with me. Get Mark and bring him with you, because he is helpful to me in my ministry." (2 Tim. 4:11, NIV®)* The biblical record of Mark's life shows a disciple turned missionary, albeit one who ran scared at least once. Let the record show that Mark did redeem himself through continued ministry or Paul would not have made sure to record his statement to Timothy shortly before his martyrdom in Rome.

(3) When was the gospel written?

Dating the gospel of Mark is a bit uncertain. While the church fathers were unanimous in testifying that Mark is the author of the gospel account bearing his name, they are not consistent regarding when he wrote it. Both Iraneaus and the Anti-Marcionite Prologue state that Mark wrote the gospel after the death of Peter (A. D. 67). A few early church fathers state that Mark wrote the gospel before Peter's death, including the Alexandrians.[7] It is also worth considering that Mark most likely would not have published the gospel that highlights the

---

[7] Wessel, Walter W. *The Expositor's Bible Commentary: Mark.* Grand Rapids, Michigan: Zondervan Publishing House. Copyright 1995. p. 7.

 Insight Bible Commentary Series

Apostle Peter's shortcomings (Mark 8:32-33, 9:5-6, 14:39-41 with 14:72, 14:37) while Peter was still alive.

Internal sources within the gospel of Mark are not conclusive. Based on Mark 13:1-2, it appears to have been written prior to A.D. 70 when the Temple in Jerusalem was destroyed by the Roman army. The disciples pointed out the magnificent structures and Jesus said, *"Do you see all these great buildings? ... Not one stone here will be left on another; every one will be thrown down."* (Mark 13:2, NIV®). Mark's account gives no indication in the narrative that the Temple was gone as Jesus had predicted. Moreover, the years leading up to this tragic event were filled with Roman persecution of Christians. Mark alludes to this persecution in the following quote from Jesus: *"Everyone will be salted with fire"* (Mark 9:49, NIV®). Nero blamed the Christians for the burning of Rome (A.D. 64). As a result, Christians were routinely arrested, tortured, and killed. One of the more gruesome execution methods was to douse the Christian with a flammable liquid and light him up as a human torch in Nero's garden.[8] The Apostle Peter himself was executed by Nero in the A.D. 64-68 time frame.[9] The early church, facing such persecution, would need a gospel account of Jesus'

---

[8] *Ibid. pp. 12-14.*
[9] *Butler. p. 920.*

persistent and strong ministry in spite of opposition and persecution.

Both the external and internal evidence point to a date on Mark's gospel in the A.D. 67-70 time frame. Mark most likely recorded sermons and sermon fragments during the ministry of the Apostle Peter. After Peter's death, Mark compiled what we now know as the gospel of Mark.

(4) What is the manuscript evidence for the gospel of Mark?

In terms of manuscript evidence, there is overwhelming support for the complete gospel of Mark as we know it today.[10] A controversy, however, has been going on since the fourth century over the true ending of Mark's gospel. The issue of where to end the Gospel of Mark will be covered in the section on Mark 16:9-20.

C. Outline and Chronology of Mark's Gospel.

The Gospel of Mark is an account of the life of Jesus shortly before His baptism through His resurrection from the

---

[10] *Lane. p. 604.*

 Insight Bible Commentary Series

dead. The following high-level outline should be helpful to guide the reader through the topics covered in Mark's gospel:

1. Overview of the Gospel of Mark (Mark 1:1).

2. Jesus Prepares For His Earthly Ministry (Mark 1:2-13).

3. Jesus Begins His Earthly Ministry in Galilee (Mark 1:14-3:35).

    a. In Capernaum (Mark 1:14-34).

    b. Traveling Through Galilee (Mark 1:35-2:12).

    c. Encountering Questions (Mark 2:13-3:6).

    d. Organizing the Disciples (Mark 3:7-35).

4. Jesus prepares His disciples (Mark 4:1-6:6).

    a. Jesus teaches His disciples through parables (Mark 4:1-34).

    b. Jesus teaches His disciples through miracles (Mark 4:35-6:6).

5. Jesus Extends His Ministry Through His Disciples (Mark 6:7-6:56).

6. Jesus encounters opposition to His ministry (Mark 7:1-8:30).

7. Jesus Moves His Ministry to Jerusalem (Mark 8:31-10:52).

a. The cost of following Jesus (Mark 8:31-9:13).

   b. The demands of faith (Mark 9:14-10:12).

   c. Finding salvation (Mark 10:13-31).

   d. Suffering and glory (Mark 10:32-52).

8. Jesus confronts Jerusalem with His authority (Mark 11:1-13:37).

   a. Presentation of the King (Mark 11:1-26).

   b. Testing of the King (Mark 11:27-12:44).

   c. Prophetic Discourse of the King on End-Time Events (Mark 13:1-37).

9. Jesus is Betrayed and Crucified (Mark 14:1-15:47).

   a. Conspiracy against Jesus (Mark 14:1-42).

   b. Arrest and Trial of Jesus (Mark 14:43-15:20).

   c. Crucifixion of Jesus (Mark 15:21-47).

10. Jesus is Vindicated By His Resurrection From the Dead (Mark 16:1-20).

From a chronological perspective, we can deduce the purpose of Mark's gospel, in part, by analyzing the amount of material used to cover the different phases of Jesus' life. There are sixteen chapters devoted to the ministry of Jesus Christ.

 Insight Bible Commentary Series

Mark devotes the following material to three primary time divisions in Jesus' life:

- Mark 1:1-8:26 covers 3 years (8 chapters).
- Mark 8:27-10:52 covers 6 months (2+ chapters).
- Mark 11:1-16:20 covers 8 days (3 chapters).

Chapters 11 through 16 cover the final week of Jesus' life. From the amount of material used we see clearly what Mark was intending to emphasize. Like a telescope, Mark's gospel broadly looks at the early ministry of Jesus, focuses in on His journey to Jerusalem, and then does a full zoom on crucifixion and resurrection of Christ. While the work of Jesus is emphasized throughout, the final week of Jesus' life is the capstone of that work.

D. Contribution of Mark's Gospel

The Gospel of Mark is unique in many respects. It is generally acknowledged as the first gospel account written. As such, Mark's gospel should be studied as the earliest account of the life of Christ. Among the four gospels, Mark is unique in that there is little unique material presented in it. Less than ten percent of Mark's gospel is not also covered in Matthew, Luke, or John. Mark's gospel is also the shortest of the four gospels. It is a brief but lively account of the life of Christ.

The focus of Mark's gospel is on the work of Jesus. No other gospel emphasizes the mighty works of Jesus Christ as found in Mark's account. His narrative describes Jesus on the move. Jesus was a mighty Servant of God even when opposed by the religious and political leaders of His day. Given the time frame of its writing, Mark surely wrote to inspire early Christians to face opposition and persecution with the same tenacity as our LORD Jesus. Mark's gospel is also a wake-up call to Christians today to get to work as Jesus did. We need to be about the Father's business, less concerned with image and form than with the actual work of carrying the gospel to a world of lost souls. As Mark concluded, we should: *"Go into all the world and preach the gospel to all creation." (Mark 16:15, NIV®)*

 Insight Bible Commentary Series

II. Jesus Prepares For His Earthly Ministry (Mark 1:2-13).

A. Jesus is announced by John the Baptist (Mark 1:2-8).

> *² as it is written in Isaiah the prophet: "I will send my messenger ahead of you, who will prepare your way"— ³ "a voice of one calling in the wilderness, 'Prepare the way for the Lord, make straight paths for him.'" ⁴ And so John the Baptist appeared in the wilderness, preaching a baptism of repentance for the forgiveness of sins. ⁵ The whole Judean countryside and all the people of Jerusalem went out to him. Confessing their sins, they were baptized by him in the Jordan River. ⁶ John wore clothing made of camel's hair, with a leather belt around his waist, and he ate locusts and wild honey. ⁷ And this was his message: "After me comes the one more powerful than I, the straps of whose sandals I am not worthy to stoop down and untie. ⁸ I baptize you with water, but he will baptize you with the Holy Spirit." (Mark 1:2-8, NIV®)*

In this passage, Mark introduces us to John the Baptist. John was the last of the Old Testament style prophets sent to proclaim the word of the LORD. The job of the prophet was to clearly identify the sins of the people, declare God's message to

 Insight Bible Commentary Series

the people, and point them to future events whereby they would know that the LORD had indeed spoken. In particular, the prophets would point forward to the Messiah or Christ who would usher in the kingdom of God. John the Baptist emerged on the Judean landscape to prepare the hearts of the people for the imminent appearance of Christ.

Parallel passages: Matthew 3:1-12; Luke 3:1-20; John 1:6-8, 1:15, 1:19-28

Mark 1:2-3: Previous prophets had predicted the ministry of John the Baptist. Note that earlier manuscripts on which the NIV®/NASB translations are based translate Mark 1:2 as *"it is written in Isaiah the prophet ..."* (NIV®). There are times where the name of a major prophet is used to represent all the Old Testament prophets. That may be what these earlier manuscripts were trying to do. But the KJV/NKJV both attribute these quotes to *"the Prophets"* because these two verses quote from both Malachi and Isaiah.

> *Behold, I send My messenger, and He will prepare the way before Me: and the Lord, whom you seek, Will suddenly come to His temple, Even the Messenger of the covenant, In whom you delight: Behold, He is coming," Says the LORD of Hosts. (Malachi 3:1, NKJV)*

> *The voice of one crying in the wilderness, "Prepare the way of the LORD; Make straight in the desert A highway for our God. (Isaiah 40:3, NKJV)*

Mark introduces John the Baptist as the messenger of God. As God's messenger, John the Baptist has instant credibility with the reader. This credibility is important because his job is to announce the coming of Christ, the Son of God whom Mark wants to explain in this gospel (Mark 1:1).

The people of Israel, chosen by God to be His light to the world, had been without a prophet for 400 years. There had been no true prophetic utterances from God, no word from the LORD to guide the people. Furthermore, though the Israelites had regrouped to form their nation once again, they were now enslaved by the Roman Empire. The people were confused about God's plan, discouraged, angry, and without hope. They lived in a spiritual wilderness.

> *And so John the Baptist appeared in the wilderness, preaching a baptism of repentance for the forgiveness of sins. (Mark 1:4, NIV®)*

Mark 1:4: It was in the spiritual wilderness, John the Baptist was called to minister the word of the LORD. Luke tells us that John grew up in the desert and there began his ministry: *"And the child grew and became strong in spirit; and he lived in the*

wilderness until he appeared publicly to Israel." (Luke 1:80, NIV®)

Like so many of the prophets before John, his life was to be a physical representation of God's spiritual reality. God often commanded prophets to perform specific object lessons that demonstrated symbolically the spiritual truth He was prophesying. For example:

- *Stand in the Temple gate*: Jeremiah was called to stand in the gates of the Temple to call the people to repentance for entering God's temple with sinful lives and sinful attitudes (Jer. 7:1-3).

- *Wear a Sash*: God told Jeremiah to wear a *"linen belt" (Jer. 13:1, NIV®)* and later hide it under a rock near the Euphrates river. The sash was ruined and useless. God gave Jeremiah this object lesson in how the prideful people who would not listen to the word of God would become marred and useless like the sash (Jer. 13:1-27).

- *A Yoke on the Neck:* Jeremiah was called by God to wear a handmade yoke around his neck as a sign that God was about to deliver Israel into the hands of *"Nebuchadnezzar king of Babylon." (Jer. 27:6, NIV®)* Later the yoke was broken in the presence of all the people to demonstrate how God would eventually deal with Babylon (Jer. 27:10).

- *Lie on the Ground for More Than a Year:* Ezekiel was to lie down before a clay mock-up of the city of

Jerusalem for 390 days and then 40 more days. This was to represent the siege of Jerusalem in the coming judgment at the hand of the Babylonians (Ezekiel 4:1-15).

- *Carry Around Packed Bags:* Ezekiel was commanded to pack some bags as for a journey. He was instructed to then carry those bags day and night before the people of Israel to show them that they would go into captivity for their sins against God and each other (Ezekiel 12:1-20).

- *Wearing a Belt Tying Both Hands Together:* The prophet Agabus demonstrated to Paul and the church that if Paul went to Jerusalem he would face imprisonment (Acts 21:10-12).

So John's preaching of God's word in the wilderness was an object lesson for the people of Israel who, at that time, were living in a spiritual wilderness. What was that lesson? John the Baptist had a powerful message for the people of his time: repentance. His message was that people should turn from their sins, confess them to God, and believe in the Christ who was coming into the world. The word of the LORD had come to them in the wilderness indicating the way out of the wilderness through repentance. Repentance is a dramatic change of mind, a change of heart deep within a person. It is like doing a "U-turn" in the road of life. Before repentance, you live life without submitting to God. After repentance, you submit your life to God.

John the Baptist bore witness to Christ. His ministry was intended to spark repentance in the hearts of the Israelites and turn them to Christ for redemption. Look at how John speaks of Christ:

- Christ the Eternal One: "*John testified concerning him. He cried out, saying, 'This is the one I spoke about when I said, "He who comes after me has surpassed me because he was before me."'*" (John 1:15, NIV®)

- Christ the Glorious One: "*'²⁶ I baptize with water,' John replied, 'but among you stands one you do not know. ²⁷ He is the one who comes after me, the straps of whose sandals I am not worthy to untie.'*" (John 1:26-27, NIV®)

- Christ the Saving One: "*²⁹ The next day John saw Jesus coming toward him and said, "Look, the Lamb of God, who takes away the sin of the world! ³⁰ This is the one I meant when I said, 'A man who comes after me has surpassed me because he was before me.' ³¹ I myself did not know him, but the reason I came baptizing with water was that he might be revealed to Israel."*" (John 1:29-31, NIV®)

- Christ the Anointed One: "*³² Then John gave this testimony: 'I saw the Spirit come down from heaven as a dove and remain on him. ³³ And I myself did not know him, but the one who sent me to baptize with water told me, "The man on whom you see the Spirit come down and remain is the one who will baptize* *with the Holy Spirit." ^{34} I have seen and I testify that this is God's Chosen One.'"* (John 1:32-34, NIV®)

- Christ the Greater One: *"He must become greater; I must become less."* (John 3:30, NIV®)

Note that John's message of repentance was given to the people before Christ began His earthly ministry. Before the time of Christ, people were saved from their sins by believing in God and in the Christ He would send into the world. Repentance is still needed today. We live in a time after Christ has come into the world and died for all our sins. We are saved by turning from our sins and believing in God and in Christ who has already come into the world.

John's mission was to prepare the nation of Israel for the coming of her King. Look at the pronouncement of the angel to John's father, Zechariah, concerning John's mission:

^{16} He will bring back many of the people of Israel to the Lord their God. ^{17} And he will go on before the Lord, in the spirit and power of Elijah, to turn the hearts of the parents to their children and the disobedient to the wisdom of the righteous—to make ready a people prepared for the Lord. (Luke 1:16-17, NIV®)

Zechariah, as High Priest of Israel, also prophesied concerning John's mission:

 Insight Bible Commentary Series

> *⁷⁶ And you, my child, will be called a prophet of the Most High; for you will go on before the Lord to prepare the way for him, ⁷⁷ to give his people the knowledge of salvation through the forgiveness of their sins, ⁷⁸ because of the tender mercy of our God, by which the rising sun will come to us from heaven ⁷⁹ to shine on those living in darkness and in the shadow of death, to guide our feet into the path of peace. (Luke 1:76-79, NIV®)*

His was a message of national repentance at an individual level. Each person needed to turn to God and away from their sins. He also pointed people to the imminent coming of Christ who would usher in the kingdom of God.

Mark 1:5: His ministry was in the *"wilderness"* (1:4), a desert region in the Holy Lands where rainfall is sparse and people are few. Typically, this term refers to the southern and eastern portions of Israel and across the Jordan River. Interestingly, the people came out to the wilderness to hear John preach. *"The whole Judean countryside and all the people of Jerusalem went out to him. Confessing their sins, they were baptized by him in the Jordan River."* (Mark 1:5, NIV®) John the Baptist had no church house, no evangelism program, no youth ministry, and no advertising program. He was simply faithful to proclaim the word of God in the power of the Holy Spirit and people came to him. The people heard God's word through John, confessed their sins and repentantly turned to God. John the Baptist was true to his name by baptizing the people in the Jordan River.

The word *"baptized"* comes from the Greek word *baptizo* which means to be overwhelmed by something. In this verse, the context is the Jordan River. The people who repentantly turned to God and Christ who was to come were overwhelmed, or immersed, in the cool water of the Jordan River. The idea of sprinkling is not conveyed by this word at all. Dyed fabric was cloth that had been *baptizo* in the dye; the suggestion of sprinkling as the primary meaning rather than immersion does not even make sense. Further, Scripture records that immediately after the baptism of Jesus He was *"coming up out of the water."* (Mark 1:10, NIV®). He was clearly immersed in the Jordan River. Many denominations disagree with the Baptist position on immersion but they do so on the basis of tradition or personal bias rather than Scripture.

The immersing baptism of John must have caused offense to the Jewish people. Typically, proselytes (non-Jews) who wished to convert to Judaism were required by the first century tradition to self-baptize themselves for ceremonial cleanness. Now, the LORD calls the Jews themselves to be baptized in preparation of the coming of Christ.

 Insight Bible Commentary Series

Mark 1:6: By today's standards, John was certainly a strange looking preacher with a very rustic church. He wore a suit of *"camel's hair, with a leather belt around his waist"* His diet consisted of *"locusts and wild honey."* The appearance and diet of John was consistent with people who lived in the desert regions of this time.

There was not much in John's ministry to attract people. His words were sharp with frequent attacks on the religious leaders: *"[7] But when he saw many of the Pharisees and Sadducees coming to where he was baptizing, he said to them: 'You brood of vipers! Who warned you to flee from the coming wrath? [8] Produce fruit in keeping with repentance.'"* (Matthew 3:7-8, NIV®) John expressed this exact same thought to the multitudes that came to be baptized by him (Luke 3:7-8). He was direct with his rebuke of the crowds, tax collectors, and even with Roman soldiers (Luke 3:10-14). This is hardly today's prescription for church growth. Yet, we see that people traveled to the wilderness to hear John proclaim the word of God with boldness and in the power of the Holy Spirit.

Many a pulpit committee would overlook a man like John the Baptist. It must have been discouraging to live in isolation, lonely to be so removed from other people, and depressing to constantly proclaim the sins of the people. Who would desire such a ministry? Nevertheless, John was faithful to do what God called him to do, even though it was not a pleasant or desirable task. God will bless you also as you remain faithful in His calling on your life, whatever and wherever that might be. No church or ministry is small or insignificant in God's sight. While John was in prison, Jesus sent the following word to him regarding his ministry: *"Truly I tell you, among those born of women there has not risen anyone greater than John the Baptist; yet whoever is least in the kingdom of heaven is greater than he."* (Matthew 11:11, NIV®) What God desires in each one of us is faithfulness to His call. Faithfulness even in an unpleasant ministry is a tremendous lesson we learn from John the Baptist.

> *[7] And this was his message: "After me comes the one more powerful than I, the straps of whose sandals I am not worthy to stoop down and untie. [8] I baptize you with water, but he will baptize you with the Holy Spirit." (Mark 1:7-8, NIV®)*

Mark 1:7-8: In his ministry, John exuded power that also drew people to hear his message. Powerful men have always attracted attention. The Bible says that John the Baptist *"[15] ... will be great in the sight of the Lord. He is never to take wine or other fermented drink, and he will be filled with the Holy Spirit even before he is born. [16] He will bring back many of the people of*

 Insight Bible Commentary Series

Israel to the Lord their God." (Luke 1:15-16, NIV®) From this description, it appears that John was also a Nazirite (Numbers 6:2-21), one who had devoted his life to serving the LORD. Abstinence from intoxicating beverages was critical to John's power; one cannot be empowered by the Holy Spirit and intoxicated at the same time: *"Do not get drunk on wine, which leads to debauchery. Instead, be filled with the Spirit."* (Ephesians 5:18, NIV®). John also ministered *"...before the Lord, in the spirit and power of Elijah, to turn the hearts of the parents to their children and the disobedient to the wisdom of the righteous—to make ready a people prepared for the Lord."* (Luke 1:17, NIV®) Elijah, was the great miracle working prophet who won a mighty battle over the false prophets of Baal (1 Kings 18:17-40). During the first century, references to all the prophets were often made by naming Elijah or Jeremiah, two of the greatest prophets of Israel (Matthew 16:14; cf. Matthew 27:9 where quotations from both Zechariah and Jeremiah are attributed to Jeremiah;). So John's coming in the spirit and power of Elias (Elijah) denotes his association with all the other prophets of God. Like all the other prophets, the power of his ministry was the Holy Spirit Himself. Likewise, your power for ministry is found when you yield yourself to the will of the Holy

Spirit. He will lead you, equip you, and empower you to accomplish His will.

The people saw John the Baptist as a mighty man, truly a prophet of God though John performed no miracle during his lifetime. Yet John pointed the people to Christ, *"One more powerful than I."* (Mark 1:7, NIV®) As powerful as John's preaching was to the people, he always pointed them to Christ as the source of his strength and the One in whom the people were to believe. John described Christ as One who possessed:

- Greater power ("*more powerful than I*").
- Greater honor ("*whose sandals I am not worthy to stoop down and untie*").
- Greater gifts ("*He will baptize you with the Holy Spirit*").

Who can baptize people with the Holy Spirit but God alone?

To the reader, John appears as a powerful man but one who needed no sword. He preached a message of submission not domination. He called people to turn to Christ and away from self. John knew that Christ the LORD possessed supreme power over all the universe. His own response to this revelation from

God (as should be ours) was to humbly repent and believe in Him.

B. Jesus is identified by God as His beloved Son (Mark 1:9-11).

> [9] *At that time Jesus came from Nazareth in Galilee and was baptized by John in the Jordan.* [10] *Just as Jesus was coming up out of the water, he saw heaven being torn open and the Spirit descending on him like a dove.* [11] *And a voice came from heaven: "You are my Son, whom I love; with you I am well pleased." (Mark 1:9-11, NIV®)*

While John the Baptist is still at work preparing the hearts of the people for the coming of Christ, Jesus arrives! He even comes to John to be baptized like any other person. However, unlike any other person, when Jesus came up out of the water God the Father identified Jesus as His beloved Son. So Jesus is identified, not only by a prophet of God -- John the Baptist -- but also by God the Father Himself. His identification reveals a close, intimate relationship as a father and son enjoy. Further, the voice from Heaven affirms Jesus as One who pleases God.

Parallel passages: Matthew 3:13-17; Luke 3:21-22; John 1:31-34

Mark 1:9: Note the geographic and chronological references given by Mark in this gospel account. He points to specific places and times in history. Far from being legend, the events Mark describes were specific and verifiable by the readers of his day. This is just another example of the uniqueness of the Bible in works of antiquity.

Why was Jesus baptized by John? John himself was surprised at Jesus' request to be baptized. But one of the reasons for Jesus' baptism was to fulfill all righteousness:

> *^{13} Then Jesus came from Galilee to the Jordan to be baptized by John. ^{14} But John tried to deter him, saying, "I need to be baptized by you, and do you come to me?" ^{15} Jesus replied, "Let it be so now; it is proper for us to do this to fulfill all righteousness." Then John consented. (Matthew 3:13-15, NIV®)*

It was right for Jesus to be baptized just like the people John exhorted in his preaching. Jesus went through this baptism to identify with sinful human beings. The baptism of Jesus identified Jesus with all humanity. Though Jesus was without sin (2 Cor. 5:21; Heb. 4:15; 1 Pet. 2:22; 1 John 3:5), He chose to relate to sinful people. Though Jesus was and is fully God (John 1:1), He also wanted to show that He was fully human. You see, God does not expect you to somehow work yourself up to

 Insight Bible Commentary Series

Heaven to have a relationship with Him. The Bible tells us that no one could ever do enough good things to make God accept you (Romans 3:20; Ephesians 2:8-9; Galatians 2:16). But God loves you so much that He brought Himself down to your level. God meets you at your own level. God comes to wherever you are. That is what Jesus Christ demonstrated in His baptism.

Mark 1:10: In Mark's gospel, you find repeated use of the words *"Just as," "as soon as," "at once,"* and *"immediately."* The Greek word *eutheos* occurs over forty times in just sixteen chapters. Mark focuses on Jesus as a Man of action, a Servant about the Father's business. Jesus is presented as confident and assured of what He must do. This is critical in the narrative because His death on the cross at the end would seem to be a failure when, in fact, it became His victory at the resurrection.

The reference *"he saw heaven being torn open"* is to Jesus who saw the reality of Heaven before Him and the Holy Spirit descending upon Him. The gospel of John records that John the Baptist also saw the Holy Spirit descend upon Jesus (John 1:33-34). Note that Jesus did not become Christ at this baptism. Many cults will attempt to spiritualize Jesus at the baptism and remove this divine empowerment prior to the cross in order to fit into their false theological framework. We know from Scripture that the angels announced to the shepherds the day Jesus was born: *"Today in the town of David a Savior has been born to you; he is the Messiah, the Lord."* (Luke 2:11, NIV®). Jesus was Christ the LORD and our Savior from eternity past to eternity future since God declared through Isaiah:

> ^{10} *"You are my witnesses," declares the Lord, "and my servant whom I have chosen, so that you may know and believe me and understand that I am he. Before me no god was formed, nor will there be one after me. ^{11} I, even I, am the Lord, and apart from me there is no savior." (Isaiah 43:10-11, NIV®)*

The Holy Spirit descended *"like a dove"* to anoint Jesus for His earthly ministry. The dove is a symbol for peace. The outworking of Jesus' ministry was and is to bring peace to the hearts of people everywhere. The world longs for peace on earth but it will not be found until there is peace inside the hearts of people everywhere. Through faith in Jesus Christ, you and I can find *"peace with God."* (Romans 5:1, NIV®)

Mark 1:11: *"And a voice came from heaven: "You are my Son, whom I love; with you I am well pleased."* (Mark 1:11, NIV®). God the Father spoke in the present tense; He did not say Jesus "will be" His Son or "was" His Son but that *"You are my Son."* Jesus is declared by God the Father to be His Son, a Son who is

 Insight Bible Commentary Series

greatly loved. So the title for Jesus, *"the Son of God"* (Mark 1:1, NIV®), refers first to His sharing the character and nature of God. This title also refers to His intimate relationship with our Heavenly Father. Jesus enjoys a Father-Son relationship with God.

This is why Jesus was able to declare to all people, "I am the way and the truth and the life. No one comes to the Father except through me." (John 14:6, NIV®). Because Jesus is God's Son, you cannot know God without accepting His Son, Jesus Christ, as your LORD and Savior.

> *[11] And this is the testimony: God has given us eternal life, and this life is in his Son. [12] Whoever has the Son has life; whoever does not have the Son of God does not have life.[13] I write these things to you who believe in the name of the Son of God so that you may know that you have eternal life. (1 John 5:11-13, NIV®).*

The phrase *"with you I am well pleased"* (Mark 1:11, NIV®) presents a key point about Jesus' life. What is it that pleases God or would cause God to say He is pleased with His Son? Only One whose life reflected His own holiness, righteousness, love, and purity. This is the mark of Jesus' life which was different that every other human that ever lived. The gospel of Mark will show how Jesus pleased the Father in every aspect of His amazing life.

Verses 10-11 also present a clear view of the three persons of the Trinity. While no single verse teaches the entirety of the doctrine of the Trinity, this is one of several verses where all three persons are mentioned simultaneously. The doctrine of the Trinity can be summarized in three major parts:

1. There is but one God [ref. Deut. 6:4; Isa. 46:9; Mal. 2:10; 1 Cor. 8:4-6; 1 Tim. 2:5; Jam. 2:19],

2. The Father [ref. 1 Chron. 29:10; Psa. 68:5, 89:6; John 5:17-18, 6:27, 13:3; 1 Cor. 1:3; Eph. 4:6], the Son [Isa. 9:6; Dan. 3:25; Matt. 1:23, 14:33, 16:16, 26:63-64; John 1:1, 10:36, 11:4; Acts 7:56, 8:37; Rom. 1:4; Heb. 1:8; 1 John 5:20; 2 John 1:9], and the Holy Spirit [Gen. 1:2; Isa. 48:16, 61:1; Matt. 12:28; Acts 5:3-4; Rom. 8:14; 1 Cor. 3:16] are each distinct from the other but each referred to as God.

3. The three are one. Mark 1:10-11 supports part 3 of the doctrine of the Trinity along with Luke 1:35 (annunciation of Jesus' birth) and Matthew 28:19 (Great Commission).

Numerous applications can be made from Mark 1:9-11:

- Consider the wonder of sinless Jesus, the Son of God, identifying with sinful people. *"God made him who*

Insight Bible Commentary Series

had no sin to be sin for us [or a *"sin offering*]", *so that in him we might become the righteousness of God."* (2 Cor. 5:21, NIV®) Jesus comes down to meet you where you are to redeem you so that you can be with Him and He can be with you forever: *"And surely I am with you always, to the very end of the age."* (Matt. 28:20, NIV®).

- Jesus is shown to be truly human, a real man who experienced life on this earth to the fullest that He might understand us completely. *"For we do not have a high priest who is unable to empathize with our weaknesses, but we have one who has been tempted in every way, just as we are—yet he did not sin."* (Heb. 4:15, NIV®)

- The old saying goes, *"The apple does not fall far from the tree."* To know God is to know His Son. To know the Son is to know God. And Jesus made it clear that He is the only way to know God (John 14:9-10) and the only way to find God (John 14:6). The beauty of the Father-Son relationship in the Trinity is that Jesus will grant that same relationship to all who trust in Him (not to become God but to have just as special a relationship with God as the Father and Son enjoy. *"[12] Yet to all who did receive him, to those who believed in his name, he gave the right to become children of God— [13] children born not of natural descent, nor of human decision or a husband's will, but born of God."* (John 1:12-13, NIV®) And *"[1] See what great love the Father has lavished on us, that we should be called children of God! And that is what we are! The reason the world does not know us is that it did not know him. [2] Dear friends, now we are children of God, and what we will be has not yet been made known. But we know that when Christ appears, we shall be like him, for we shall see him as he is."* (1 John 3:1-2, NIV®)

C. Jesus overcomes temptation in the wilderness (Mark 1:12-13).

¹² At once the Spirit sent him out into the wilderness, ¹³ and he was in the wilderness forty days, being tempted by Satan. He was with the wild animals, and angels attended him. (Mark 1:12-13, NIV®)

After Jesus' baptism, He is driven by the Spirit into the wilderness for a time of prayer and fasting prior to beginning His earthly ministry. He is also tested severely by the devil for forty days. Mark emphasizes the drive for His ministry was the Holy Spirit. The danger through His ministry was the devil and the world. Jesus is shown to be a mighty Servant of God by overcoming both threats.

Parallel passages: Matthew 4:1-11; Luke 4:1-13

Mark 1:12: Again we see *"At once"* used to indicate the urgency of Jesus' life. As soon as the baptism and anointing by the Holy Spirit was complete, Jesus was driven to this time of preparation and testing. *"The Spirit"* is the Holy Spirit who *"sent"* (compelled) Jesus to follow this course. Jesus could follow no course but the Father's will. Being fully God, He knew what He

 Insight Bible Commentary Series

had to do. Being fully man, He was led by the Spirit of God throughout His life. Being marked for ministry, Jesus was immediately tested.

Mark 1:13: What was Jesus doing *"in the wilderness forty days?"* One reason for this time alone was to fast and pray, seeking the Father's will (Matthew 4:2,4). Jesus had to settle many questions such as where to go, when to go, what to say, how to respond to both criticism and success. The second reason was to be *"tempted by Satan."*

Now God cannot be tempted to sin. *"When tempted, no one should say, 'God is tempting me.' For God cannot be tempted by evil, nor does he tempt anyone."* (James 1:13, NIV®). The Greek word *peirazomai* translated *"tempted"* can also mean to test, to try, or to prove. This is what was happening to Jesus. He was being tested to prove His authenticity. Further, the passages in Matthew and Luke provide details of Jesus' encounter with the devil during this time. The devil's goading words, *"If you are the Son of God,"* (Mat. 4:3,6; Luke 4:3,9, NIV®) were a taunt since the conditional phrase indicates the statement is in fact true. We might say today: "If you are the Son of God, and you are, then turn the stones to bread." Like the melting of a gold nugget to prove its genuineness, Jesus' time with the devil was a proving ground to show that He was indeed the Son of God.

When the Holy Spirit calls you into the ministry, you commit yourself to serving the LORD. You also present yourself to the devil as though there were a big target sign on your chest saying *"beat me up!"* The devil will test you as at no other time in your life than when you are first called. The purpose is to break you. If he can do so early enough in your call, he can get you to doubt that the LORD ever revealed His will to you in regard to the ministry. Never allow yourself to believe the difficulties you face indicate that God made a mistake. Nor should you think the hard times indicate that God despises you or somehow thinks you unfit for duty. No, but God does use such times to hone and refine our faith for greater ministry:

> [5] *And have you completely forgotten this word of encouragement that addresses you as a father addresses his son? It says, "My son, do not make light of the Lord's discipline, and do not lose heart when he rebukes you,* [6] *because the Lord disciplines the one he loves, and he chastens everyone he accepts as his son."* [7] *Endure hardship as discipline; God is treating you as his children. For what children are not disciplined by their father?* [8] *If you are not disciplined—and everyone undergoes discipline—then you are not legitimate, not true sons and daughters at all.* [9] *Moreover, we have all had human fathers who*

 Insight Bible Commentary Series

disciplined us and we respected them for it. How much more should we submit to the Father of spirits and live! (Heb. 12:5-9, NIV®)

The devil can never win if you lean with all your weight on the LORD Jesus Christ. *"You, dear children, are from God and have overcome them, because the one who is in you is greater than the one who is in the world."* (1 John 4:4, NIV®) Know with certainty the One who called you to be a minister of reconciliation (2 Cor. 5:18-19) and you will never be swept away by the enemies of god, *"for God's gifts and his call are irrevocable."* (Rom. 11:29, NIV®)

D. Conclusion of Section 2.

Jesus, the Son of God, is now prepared to begin His earthly ministry. A mighty prophet of God announced His arrival. God the Father announced His relationship with Jesus. And the wilderness experience proved these two announcements were true. The mighty servant of God was ready to change the world.

To run any race, one must be prepared to win (1 Cor. 9:24). Otherwise, why run the race? For the ministry, one must get prepared through an understanding of your call, a honing of your gifts, and proving time to demonstrate the reality of God's work in your life and ministry. Jesus took time to prepare. So must you and I if we are to be mighty servants of God. Education, such as you can receive through a Christ-centered, Bible-teaching Seminary, is vital to helping you understand and hone your gifts for ministry, especially in the preaching and teaching of God's word. Get the best education you can afford and the most education you are capable of attaining. Education may seem to be laborious and long. But a wise pastor once counseled me to prioritize in the short-term that which will yield the greatest long-term benefit. Education will position you for maximum ministry for the rest of your life.

> *[1] Therefore, since we are surrounded by such a great cloud of witnesses, let us throw off everything that hinders and the sin that so easily entangles. And let us run with perseverance the race marked out for us, [2] fixing our eyes on Jesus, the pioneer and perfecter of faith. For the joy set before him he endured the cross, scorning its shame, and sat down at the right hand of the throne of God. [3] Consider him who endured such opposition from sinners, so that you will not grow weary and lose heart. (Heb. 12:1-3, NIV®)*

 Insight Bible Commentary Series

III. Jesus Begins His Earthly Ministry in Galilee (Mark 1:14-3:35)

A. In Capernaum (Mark 1:14-34).

(1) Jesus proclaims the message of His ministry (Mark 1:14-15).

> *¹⁴ After John was put in prison, Jesus went into Galilee, proclaiming the good news of God. ¹⁵ "The time has come," he said. "The kingdom of God has come near. Repent and believe the good news!" (Mark 1:14-15, NIV®)*

Shortly after Jesus' baptism, John was imprisoned by King Herod (we will cover the reason for this later in chapter six). Jesus then came out of the wilderness proclaiming the central message of His ministry: The kingdom of God is here. Jesus had a right to proclaim such a message. Unlike a prophet or a preacher, Jesus not only gave the message but He was the message. He commanded the people to repent and believe the good news.

Parallel passages: Matthew 4:12-17; Luke 4:14-15

Mark 1:14-15: Galilee was both the beginning point of Jesus' ministry as well as being His base of operations. Galilee is the northern region of modern-day Israel, surrounding the Sea of

 Insight Bible Commentary Series

Galilee. The town of Capernaum, in Galilee, was the place where He and His disciples would gather for rest and refreshment at the home of Andrew and Simon Peter (Mark 1:29). This fulfilled the promise of God through the prophet Isaiah:

> [1] *Nevertheless, there will be no more gloom for those who were in distress. In the past he humbled the land of Zebulun and the land of Naphtali, but in the future he will honor Galilee of the nations, by the Way of the Sea, beyond the Jordan—* [2] *The people walking in darkness have seen a great light; on those living in the land of deep darkness a light has dawned. (Isaiah 9:1-2, NIV®)*

The gospel, as explained earlier, means good news. To a people oppressed from without by the Roman government and burdened within by sin, the coming of the Kingdom of God was indeed good news.

A kingdom is the rule of a king extended over a particular area and/or a group of people. The Bible speaks of the *"kingdom of God"* (Mark 1:15, NIV®) in several ways. First, it can refer to the rule of God in one's life: "[20] *Once, on being asked by the Pharisees when the kingdom of God would come, Jesus replied, "The coming of the kingdom of God is not something that can be observed,* [21] *nor will people say, 'Here it is,' or 'There it is,' because the kingdom of God is in your midst."* (Luke 17:20-21, NIV®) The Apostle Paul described it this way: *"[17]For the kingdom of God is not a matter of eating and drinking, but of righteousness, peace and joy in the Holy Spirit, [18] because anyone who serves Christ in this way is pleasing to God and receives human approval."* (Romans 14:17-18, NIV®)

Second, the *"kingdom of God"* (Mark 1:15, NIV®) can refer to the literal kingdom on Earth that God promised to Israel (Isaiah 9:6-7; 11:1-16) and the disciples expected. Just prior to Jesus' ascension to Heaven we read: *"[6] Then they gathered around him and asked him, "Lord, are you at this time going to restore the kingdom to Israel?" [7] He said to them: "It is not for you to know the times or dates the Father has set by his own authority."* (Acts 1:6-7, NIV®) This kingdom on Earth will be fulfilled in the Millennial Kingdom (Rev. 20:4) because God always keeps His word.

The third way the phrase *"kingdom of God"* (Mark 1:15, NIV®) is used is to refer to God's sovereign rule over all things in Heaven and on Earth: *"Yours, Lord, is the greatness and the power and the glory and the majesty and the splendor, for everything in heaven and earth is yours. Yours, Lord, is the kingdom; you are exalted as head over all."* (1 Chron. 29:11, NIV®, also 1 Cor. 15:24-28). In Mark, the *"kingdom of God"*

 Insight Bible Commentary Series

(Mark 1:15, NIV®) refers primarily to the rule of God in the heart and life of the individual. Repentance and belief are activities of an individual, not a nation. Is your life committed to God? Are you trusting Him enough to follow Jesus? Does God and His standard of righteousness rule in your life, your family, your school, your church, and your work place?

Note also that no person will hear the gospel of the kingdom of God except through the ""*proclaiming.*" (Mark 1:14, NIV®) As the Bible states: "How, then, can they call on the one they have not believed in? And how can they believe in the one of whom they have not heard? And how can they hear without someone preaching to them?" (Romans 10:14, NIV®) The Bible goes on to state: "*Consequently, faith comes from hearing the message, and the message is heard through the word about Christ.*" (Romans 10:17, NIV®) The weight of New Testament teaching firmly declares the need for every person to exercise personal faith in Jesus Christ. Because Jesus is unique -- both human and divine -- each person must acknowledge Jesus as LORD and Savior. And every person must hear the preaching of the gospel in order to be saved. Jesus faithfully proclaimed this message throughout His ministry. Let this same urgency to share the gospel be upon every Christian!

Mark 1:15: *"The time has come"* (NIV®). God's plan of redemption was prepared before the world was created (Eph. 1:3-4; 1 Pet. 1:20; Rev. 13:8). God neither caused Adam's sin, nor was He surprised by it. God had a plan to redeem sinful people before Adam took his first breath. And from the beginning, God made His plan of redemption known:

- **A Deliverer** who would deal with sin and the devil (Gen. 3:15).

- **A Descendent of Abraham** who would bless all people (Gen. 22:18).

- **A Prophet** to be listened to and obeyed (Deut. 18:18-19).

- **A Suffering Servant** who would bear the sins of all people (Isa. 53:5-6).

- **A Savior** who would die (Dan. 9:26) but will rise again (Psalm 16:8-11).

- **A Covenant-Maker** offering forgiveness of sins and new life (Jer. 31:31-34).

Jesus' earthly ministry proclaimed the fulfillment of God's plan. The time of the Savior was fulfilled. God is faithful to do everything He promised. And so the kingdom of God *"has come near."* (Mark 1:15, NIV®) The rule and reign of God is nearer now than ever before. God has come to the Earth in the

flesh (John 1:1,14) to proclaim His redemption message in person. God spoke:

> *[1] In the past God spoke to our ancestors through the prophets at many times and in various ways, [2] but in these last days he has spoken to us by his Son, whom he appointed heir of all things, and through whom also he made the universe. [3] The Son is the radiance of God's glory and the exact representation of his being, sustaining all things by his powerful word. After he had provided purification for sins, he sat down at the right hand of the Majesty in heaven. (Hebrews 1:1-3, NIV®)*

The phrase *"has come near"* (Mark 1:15, NIV®) means nearby and very close. Through the Holy Spirit, we today also find *"[8] But what does it say? "The word is near you; it is in your mouth and in your heart," that is, the message concerning faith that we proclaim: [9] If you declare with your mouth, "Jesus is Lord," and believe in your heart that God raised him from the dead, you will be saved."* (Romans 10:8-9, NIV®) God has not made it impossible to know Him or to find redemption. He reached down from eternity into time to offer salvation to every person. The ministry of Jesus was to proclaim this great message in full living color. Someone has called Jesus *"love with skin on."* Speaking as a man in human language on a level that a child can comprehend, Jesus communicated the good news of the kingdom to a fallen world desperate for meaning and fulfillment.

Jesus said to *"Repent and believe the good news!"* (Mark 1:15, NIV®) John's message of repentance pointed forward to Christ. Now Jesus Christ has come and He proclaims the reality of the gospel. If repentance is like a U-turn, then believing is taking the first step in the new direction. The word *"believe"* translates the Greek word *pisteuo* which embodies the meaning of three words: affirm, trust, and commit. One affirms the truth of the gospel, trusts in the person and work of Jesus Christ, and commits one's life to Him. You cannot take away any one of these components without completely changing the meaning of the word *"believe"* as used in Mark 1:15.

Jesus said that you should repent. Repent from what? He means a complete turn in your belief about Jesus Christ. Rather than believe He is just a man, or a great teacher, or a prophet, you must believe that He is the Son of God who came to this Earth as a perfect man. Jesus also said you should believe in the gospel. What is His gospel? That He came to this Earth to offer Himself as a sacrifice for your sins. Jesus took the penalty of your sins upon Himself! Three days later, He rose from the grave to prove He is our LORD and Savior (1 Cor. 15:3-4).

Now to many, the gospel is unbelievable. That God would care at all about sinners is unthinkable. That God would give His only begotten Son as a ransom for sinners is unheard.

Yet, this is precisely what Jesus communicated in His teaching and on the cross at Calvary. That is why the gospel is such good news.

With this direct, straightforward declaration, Jesus begins His ministry in Galilee. The offer of redemption is made to all who will believe the gospel.

(2) Jesus calls His first disciples (Mark 1:16-20).

> *[16] As Jesus walked beside the Sea of Galilee, he saw Simon and his brother Andrew casting a net into the lake, for they were fishermen. [17] "Come, follow me," Jesus said, "and I will send you out to fish for people." [18] At once they left their nets and followed him. [19] When he had gone a little farther, he saw James son of Zebedee and his brother John in a boat, preparing their nets. [20] Without delay he called them, and they left their father Zebedee in the boat with the hired men and followed him. (Mark 1:16-20, NIV®)*

As Jesus moves through Galilee, He invites two sets of brothers to be His disciples. Over the course of three and a half years, Jesus will teach, model, and mentor these unschooled men in the truth of God's word and His plan of redemption. It is noteworthy that each of these four men immediately left behind their family and business to follow Jesus.

Parallel passages: Matthew 4:18-22; Luke 5:1-11

Mark 1:16: The first two brothers called by Jesus were Simon and Andrew. They had a fishing business on the Sea of Galilee. Simon is known as Simon Peter, who later became the chief spokesman for the disciples of Jesus. The Sea of Galilee was known for an abundance of fish, the only freshwater lake in the area. Located 700 feet below the Mediterranean Sea and surrounded by mountains, the Sea of Galilee was also known for sudden, violent storms. Therefore, those who made their living as fishermen were rough but courageous souls.

Mark 1:17: Jesus said to Simon and Andrew, *"follow Me."* (Mark 1:17, NIV®) Jesus' call to them was personal and required great sacrifice. They had to leave their livelihood, the family business at that, their family, and their friends. Jesus commanded them to follow Him. This is the nature of Jesus' call to each of us today: *"follow Me."* (Mark 1:17, NIV®) It is not a complicated command at all but it is compelling. Jesus later said, *"Whoever wants to be my disciple must deny themselves and take up their cross daily and follow me."* (Luke 9:23, NIV®). As we will see in Mark's gospel, Jesus is One who is all-knowing, all-powerful, with love that is undying. While it may be hard to set aside your own will and desires to follow Jesus, you do so knowing in full confidence that you follow a LORD

who is good to the core, wise beyond our ability to comprehend, loving, righteous, just, and true all of the time. Though the path may be difficult, such a leader is easy to follow.

Note that it is Jesus who *"will send you out to fish for people."* (Mark 1:17, NIV®) Using an analogy familiar to these fishermen, Jesus reveals the type of ministry they would undertake: evangelism. The gospel would be proclaimed to bring people into the kingdom of God like fish into a net. The good news is attractive to those receptive to God's general revelation through His creation (Psalm 19:1-4; Romans 1:19-20) and through our conscience (Romans 2:14-16; 1 Tim. 1:19). If one responds positively to God's general revelation, the good news will bring both conviction of sin and rejoicing in our Savior, Jesus Christ. Jesus also indicates that He is the power source for evangelism. It is the work of Jesus to make believers become as fishers of men, not through one's own work. Make it a priority in your life to seek Him and through your life seek to lift up the name of Jesus. The result of your life will be a net full of men, women, and children who embrace our LORD and Savior, Jesus Christ, and enter into the kingdom of God.

Mark 1:18: The Bible records that the two brothers immediately followed Jesus. Luke records, *"So they pulled their boats up on* *shore, left everything and followed him."* (Luke 5:11, NKJV) The call of Jesus on one's life is direct, personal, and compelling. The text says, *"Without delay He called them"* (Mark 1:20, NIV®) and *"At once they left their nets and followed Him."* (Mark 1:18, NIV®)

Mark 1:19: Two more brothers, James and John, are called by Jesus. They are the sons of Zebedee, apparently the owner of the fishing business (Mark 1:20). Along with Simon Peter, they became part of the inner circle of Jesus' disciples. While Jesus taught the disciples openly, these three consulted with Jesus privately and Jesus showed them things He did not invite the others to see such as the raising of Jairus' daughter (Mark 5:37; Luke 8:51), His transfiguration (Mark 9:2), the Olivet Discourse (Mark 13:3), and His mournful praying the night before He went to the cross (Matthew 26:37). Simon, Andrew, James, and John were all partners in the fishing business (Luke 5:10), a common practice during this time.

The demand of discipleship is obedience with urgency. It is easy to say you follow Jesus but do nothing for the kingdom of God. Churches are filled with people who come to church but do not follow Jesus. This may seem to be the easy approach but is not true discipleship. Jesus clearly taught, *"[31] To the Jews who had believed him, Jesus said, "If you hold to my teaching, you*

are really my disciples. ³² Then you will know the truth, and the truth will set you free." (John 8:31-32, NIV®) The only truth that sets you free is the truth that is obeyed. These four men obeyed the call to discipleship and did so with urgency. No matter the cost, the most important thing in the world is to follow Jesus. Your effectiveness in ministry will be in direct proportion to the urgency of your obedience to the call of Christ.

The demand is not without reward. Let us never forget the care and concern God has for those who love Him and follow Jesus. The Psalmist wrote:

> *1 Praise the Lord, my soul; all my inmost being, praise his holy name. 2 Praise the Lord, my soul, and forget not all his benefits— 3 who forgives all your sins and heals all your diseases, 4 who redeems your life from the pit and crowns you with love and compassion, 5 who satisfies your desires with good things so that your youth is renewed like the eagle's. (Psalms 103:1-5, NIV®)*

Jesus made it clear that if we seek to follow Him, He will meet all our needs: *"But seek first his kingdom and his righteousness, and all these things will be given to you as well."* (Matthew 6:33, NIV®) Moreover, Jesus came to give us not only eternal life but abundant life in the here and now (John 10:10). The writer of Hebrews also reminds us of the pleasure

God has in our obedience: *"And do not forget to do good and to share with others, for with such sacrifices God is pleased."* (Heb. 13:16, NIV®) Sharing with others is the hallmark of Christian virtues, no greater a witness to the world of the love of God. So your obedience to Jesus Christ is not in vain. There is great reward in this life and in the one to come (Mark 10:29-30).

So the message of Jesus' ministry is proclaimed (Mark 1:14-15) and the ministry team is organized (Mark 1:16-20). Now Jesus will demonstrate His power and authority to the world.

(3) Jesus commands authority over demons (Mark 1:21-28).

> [21] *They went to Capernaum, and when the Sabbath came, Jesus went into the synagogue and began to teach.* [22] *The people were amazed at his teaching, because he taught them as one who had authority, not as the teachers of the law.* [23] *Just then a man in their synagogue who was possessed by an impure spirit cried out,* [24] *"What do you want with us, Jesus of Nazareth? Have you come to destroy us? I know who you are—the Holy One of God!"* [25] *"Be quiet!" said Jesus sternly. "Come out of him!"* [26] *The impure spirit shook the man violently and came out of him with a shriek.* [27] *The people were all so amazed that they asked each other, "What is this? A new teaching—and with authority! He even gives orders to impure spirits and they obey him."* [28] *News about him spread*

 Insight Bible Commentary Series

quickly over the whole region of Galilee. (Mark 1:21-28, NIV®)

On the first Sabbath since beginning His earthly ministry, Jesus enters the Synagogue to teach the word of God. It astonishes the crowd that His message does not rely on the testimony and interpretation of other Rabbi's as was the custom during this time. Rather, Jesus teaches the Scriptures as though He was the One who wrote them (as a matter of fact, He did!). A demon-possessed man confronts Jesus. The demons reveal Jesus' identity as the Holy One of God. Jesus rebukes and drives out the demon thereby confirming the authority of His teaching. News of this miracle-working Teacher spread quickly throughout the region of Galilee.

Mark 1:21: Immediately on the Sabbath, Jesus began teaching. People gathered in synagogues to hear God's word. This was an important time in their lives. The synagogue was a local place of worship for the Jewish people. While the Temple in Jerusalem was to be the central focus of worship, not everyone could make the journey there. In the Old Testament, Psalm 74:8 appears to reference such a place, though worship outside of the Temple was generally discouraged because it was associated with the pagan religions. Synagogues seem to have emerged after the destruction of Solomon's temple in 586 B.C. in order to maintain the teaching of the Law and the identity of the Jewish people wherever they were scattered. Wherever a town had at least ten Jewish men, a synagogue was formed.

The NIV® omits the word *"immediately"* (from the Greek "eutheos") but it is found in the underlying texts for the KJV/NKJV. *"Immediately"* indicates the importance of what Jesus did on this Sabbath. In the synagogue, Jesus immediately met them at their point of need -- the need to hear God's word.

Mark 1:22: The people were *"amazed"* at Jesus' teaching. The word *"amazed"* is derived from a Greek word that means *"to be struck."* The truth that Jesus proclaimed was so amazing compared to what they had been taught before it was as though the truth reached out and slapped them in the face. What was so amazing about Jesus' teaching? First, He spoke the very word of God. While the Torah (the first five books of the Old Testament) was read each Sabbath, and still is today in Jewish synagogues, the sermons that followed relied upon prior rabbinical traditions and interpretations. The "authority" of the scribes was rooted in words of other men. Jesus taught and explained the word of God by His own authority. In addition, Jesus used stories, figures of speech, and illustrations from everyday life to explain and apply the word of God. While Mark does not highlight this aspect of Jesus' teaching, we see it clearly in the other three gospels. Mark

 Insight Bible Commentary Series

focuses on the works, not the words, of Jesus. Yet, the other gospel accounts show that Jesus was the preeminent expository preacher.

Would the preaching and teaching of God's word be something new in your church? How unfortunate today that so many people are surprised when a preacher boldly proclaims the word of God! This reveals a glaring deficiency of expository preaching in body of Christ. Understand that expository preaching is not simply a running commentary on Scripture. Rather, expository preaching clearly reveals the truth of God's word and exposes the meaning with application to the particular congregation. We see this not only in the teaching of Jesus but in the Old Testament as well. Ezra led the congregation in the public reading of God's word while:

> [7] *The Levites—Jeshua, Bani, Sherebiah, Jamin, Akkub, Shabbethai, Hodiah, Maaseiah, Kelita, Azariah, Jozabad, Hanan and Pelaiah—instructed the people in the Law while the people were standing there.* [8] *They read from the Book of the Law of God, making it clear and giving the meaning so that the people understood what was being read. (Nehemiah 8:7-8, NIV®)*

In Jesus' Sermon on the Mount (Matthew, chapters 5-7), we see frequent use of *"You have heard that it was said..."*

(NIV®) citing an Old Testament law. Jesus would then explain the true meaning and intent of that law followed by a real-life application that the people could understand (Matthew 5:21-24; 5:27-30; 5:31-32; 5:33-37; 5:38-42; 5:43-48). This is expository preaching at its best: explain, interpret, and apply the word of God. The word proclaimed by Jesus *"had authority"* (Matthew 7:29, NIV®) in that it could not be refuted. Where does your authority come from when preaching or teaching the word of God? It comes from exposing the clear truth of God's word. When you stick to the main truth of a passage of Scripture with clear explanation and relevant application of that truth to the lives of your congregation, no one will be able to refute your word either. People may still object to what you say but the expository approach allows you to simply point them back to God's word as your authority.

In the synagogue, the people *"were amazed at his teaching."* (Mark 1:22, NIV®) This usually happens when God speaks. Be faithful in proclaiming God's word to your congregation. God has promised that His word will not return void but will accomplish His purpose (Isaiah 55:10-11). But it must be His word and not your own, His truth and not your own. Also, your authority rests solely in God whose word is to be trusted (Psalm 119:42) and lasts forever:

 Insight Bible Commentary Series

The grass withers and the flowers fall, but the word of our God endures forever. (Isaiah 40:8, NIV®)

As long as you clearly communicate His truth with application, God's people will be blessed with spiritual strength and growth.

Mark 1:23-24: As Jesus enters the synagogue in Galilee (Mark 1:21), He encounters a man *"possessed by an impure spirit."* Here *"spirit"* refers to an angelic creature that is a created being but without a physical body. Angels were originally created by God with some form of personal will or choice. The Bible reveals that one-third of the angels made an irrevocable choice to rebel against God and follow another rebellious angel, Satan (Rev. 12:3-4). Hence, the fallen angels are what we call *demons*. The rendering *"possessed by an impure spirit"* (NIV®) is a misnomer as applied to demons and humans because demons do not possess anything but hatred toward God. The term *demon-possession* refers to the influence of one or more demons upon an individual. The work of demons is to steal, kill, and deceive people (John 8:44; 10:10). Demons can exercise a great degree of control of people through various forms of manipulation. This control can increase when one willfully turns away from God.

This man was so controlled by the demons that they even controlled his speech.

What was a demon-possessed man doing in the Synagogue? Either the religious leaders allowed him into the synagogue in order to test Jesus or he was a regular guest. If the latter is true, then this synagogue had some real problems. Evidently, the word of God was not being proclaimed with clarity and conviction. Jesus had a forceful label for the synagogue where people claimed the Law and a religious heritage of Judaism but had no faith to back it up:

> *I know your afflictions and your poverty—yet you are rich! I know about the slander of those who say they are Jews and are not, but are a synagogue of Satan. (Rev. 2:9, NIV®, ref. also Rev. 3:9)*

What happened when the demons that possessed this poor man came into the presence of Jesus Christ? They confronted Jesus with His true identity:

> *[23] ... a man ... cried out, [24] "What do you want with us, Jesus of Nazareth? Have You come to destroy us? I know who You are—the Holy One of God!" (Mark 1:23-24, NIV®)*

First, consider the concerns of the demons. If you understand these concerns, you can also understand how easily

 Insight Bible Commentary Series

people can be manipulated and influenced to do the work of Satan:

> *"What do you want with us"* – The demons revealed the reality of their rebellion against God. They are selfish. This concern illustrates that they do not want God to interfere with their evil plans. People today have a saying that they want to "do their own thing." Little do they realize that selfishness is the devil's work. Like so many people, they try to live their own life without God involved in it, keeping God at arm's length as it were. The demons declare plainly that they have no intention of following God's will on their own. Their work is decidedly unholy.

> *"Have You come to destroy us?"* – The demons realize their fate is sealed. They just do not know when God will exercise His final judgment upon them. Until then, they live in fear of His wrath. Is it not ironic that they fear the judgment of God but do not fear God Himself? They will also encourage this same fear of God in people. This fear of judgment keeps many people from seeking the grace and forgiveness of the LORD.

> *"I know who You are"* – Further irony is found that although they know God is real they fail to love or obey Him. A common myth in this time was that in knowing someone's true identity allowed you to exercise some level of control over the person. Apparently the demons thought this statement might give them some level of control over Jesus. Obviously, they were unsuccessful.

Moreover, Jesus could speak for Himself and did not need nor did He desire the testimony of demons as to His true identity. For these reasons, Jesus rebuked the demons.

So many people today try to live with these same concerns, not realizing they are unwittingly being influenced by the forces of Satan. The result is an empty life. Unfortunately, many pursue further selfish and unholy endeavors in an attempt to fill the emptiness. An empty life becomes filled with despair, anger, depression, and waste. Demonic control is quite easy if Satan can deceive one with the lies in this verse.

It is noteworthy, though, that even the demons, the enemies of God, declare Jesus to be *"the Holy One of God!"* (Mark 1:23-24, NIV®) The demons do not trust in Jesus Christ as LORD but they acknowledge that Jesus Christ is LORD. Take note of how the phrase *"Holy One"* is used. In the Old Testament, the LORD God is called the *"Holy One"* (Job 6:10; Isaiah 40:25, NIV®) or the *"Holy One of Israel"* (Psalm 78:41, NIV®). Look also in Psalm 71: *"I will praise you with the harp for your faithfulness, my God; I will sing praise to you with the lyre, Holy One of Israel."* (Psalm 71:22, NIV®). It is the LORD God who is called the "Holy One" or the "Holy One of Israel." This is a clear reference to the deity of Christ by no less than the demons themselves. It is possible to know a fact but not trust in

that fact. It is possible to believe the fact about someone without believing in someone. Here we see that the demons know the identity of Jesus but they do not believe in Jesus. As a result, the demons will one day be cast into Hell to receive eternal punishment (Matt. 25:41).

Mark 1:25-26: Jesus mercifully drove the demons out of the man. His instruction to the demons to conceal His true identity was two-fold: (1) Jesus did not need the help of demons to accomplish His mission and (2) Jesus did not desire emphasis on His identity as Messiah too early in His ministry. Why would Jesus not want people to know He was the Messiah? Many have called this issue the *Messianic Secret* in the Gospel of Mark. Part of the speculation is that Mark's gospel is an apology for why the Jews as a nation rejected Him as their Messiah. Further speculation is that Mark was creating intrigue for his readers who wanted to know the true identity of Jesus. Neither of these theories is satisfactory since in the very first verse Mark declares the identity of Jesus plainly: *"Jesus the Messiah, the Son of God."* (Mark 1:1, NIV®)

The truth is that if people realized early on He was the long awaited Messiah, they would no doubt attempt to make Him king by force. The notion of Messiah during this time was that of a political leader who would crush the enemies of Israel and restore her former greatness. In spite of Jesus' effort to gradually reveal His identity, there were times where the people tried to crown Him king (John 6:15 after feeding the five thousand with a small quantity of fish and bread; John 12:12-19 in His triumphal entry to Jerusalem after the resurrection of Lazarus). Jesus knew that revealing His identity too soon would interfere with His ability to freely proclaim the kingdom of God. It would also force the hand of the religious and political community to move against Him immediately, further hindering His mission. Jesus preached the word of God, ministered to people out of compassion and to confirm the truth of His message, and slowly revealed His identity in both word and deed. This was the Father's will to get the gospel of the kingdom out to as many people as possible in and around Israel during His earthly ministry.

Mark 1:27-28: The people's reaction to Jesus' miracles shows their intended effect: they recognized the authority of Jesus' words. The people were truly amazed at the "new" teaching accompanied by "new" powers at work. While the preaching of God's word should not be considered a new thing, it often is new to congregations with pastors that substitute "feel-good" messages, entertainment, and pop psychology for serious

expository preaching. The reaction to God's truth accompanied by God's miracles is understandable: Jesus' fame spread "quickly" throughout the region of Galilee.

The promise of miracles has always attracted a crowd. From Oral Roberts to Benny Hinn, so-called miracle-workers make extravagant claims of their ability to heal people. As we see in Jesus' ministry, the focus of the miracles is to authenticate the truth of the preacher's words. Today we have the word of God confirmed by the ultimate miracle: the resurrection of Jesus Christ from the dead. As a preacher, teacher, evangelist, or missionary, you proclaim the very word of God based on the resurrection of our LORD Jesus Christ. Can God perform miracles today? Since God is all-powerful, He can perform any miracle that does not violate His righteousness. Stories from the mission field are replete with miraculous signs from God. In a culture with no Bible in the language of that people group, miracles may be used by God to authenticate the words of the missionary. It must be clear, however, that it is not the power of the missionary but of God to whom the missionary testifies.

Jesus, the Son of God, has now demonstrated His authority in teaching. He is the One to whom we should listen. Also, Jesus demonstrated authority over the demonic spirit-world. He is a force who cannot be ignored. Next, Jesus turns to physical illness.

(4) Jesus commands power over sickness (Mark 1:29-31).

> ^{29} *As soon as they left the synagogue, they went with James and John to the home of Simon and Andrew.* ^{30} *Simon's mother-in-law was in bed with a fever, and they immediately told Jesus about her.* ^{31} *So he went to her, took her hand and helped her up. The fever left her and she began to wait on them. (Mark 1:29-31, NIV®)*

After driving out demons from a man in the synagogue, Jesus and the disciples enter Simon's house. Simon's mother-in-law was sick with a fever. Jesus healed her immediately and so completely that she was able to rise up and serve them. This healing is one of many to demonstrate Jesus' power over sickness.

Mark 1:29: Jesus and His four disciples left the synagogue and went straight to Simon's house. Simon lived there with his wife, her mother, and Andrew, his brother. Presumably they gathered there for fellowship and refreshment.

Mark 1:30: Simon's mother-in-law had a fever serious enough to keep her in bed. During the first century there were no miracle pills for fever like aspirin, Advil, or Tylenol. Such an

Insight Bible Commentary Series

illness might easily have been life-threatening. In such a situation, the disciples went to Jesus and told Him of her illness. Curiously, they did not ask Him to heal her nor did they beg. Note that they simply let Him know of the need.

Mark 1:31: Mark presents several details about the healing, departing from his usually terse, concise narrative. Jesus came to her as she lay in bed. He took her by the hand, giving her a personal touch. Then He lifted her up out of the bed. The fever left at once – the original Greek text includes "euqewV" meaning *"immediately."* What a beautiful picture of Jesus' up-close and personal love for people! He could have snapped His fingers from where He sat and healed Simon's mother-in-law. Instead, He came to her. He touched her, held her, and lifted her up. The LORD Jesus is not some far off, far out deity who does not care. He gets up-close and person in His love for you.

This healing also gives us an important example in the healing power of touch. Though we do not command sickness away, as Jesus our LORD was able to do, we can provide comfort and strength to those who are sick through a personal touch. As you hear of sick friends, and especially family members (1 Tim. 3:5,5:4,5:8), make it a point to visit them in person. Be sure to offer a personal touch such as a hug or holding their hand or patting them on the back. You will give more comfort to them by this personal touch than by anything else you could say or do.

The remarkable thing about this situation is that the woman who was sick became the woman who served. *"And she began to wait on them."* (Mark 1:31, NIV®). Jesus healed her so completely that she was ready to work. No lingering effects of the fever remained. You could look at this as a wonderful picture of salvation. Jesus takes you from being sick with sin, unable to do anything worthwhile for the kingdom of God, to being completely healed of the penalty and power of sin, able to serve the living God. *"For we are God's handiwork, created in Christ Jesus to do good works, which God prepared in advance for us to do."* (Eph. 2:10, NIV®).

Jesus has now demonstrated His remarkable power over sickness in addition to the demonic realm.

(5) Jesus commands power over all who are sick (Mark 1:32-34).

> *^{32} That evening after sunset the people brought to Jesus all the sick and demon-possessed. ^{33} The whole town gathered at the door, ^{34} and Jesus healed many who had various diseases. He also drove out many demons, but he would not let the*

 Insight Bible Commentary Series

demons speak because they knew who he was. (Mark 1:32-34, NIV®)

After healing Simon's mother-in-law, Jesus' reputation grows dramatically. Waiting until the Sabbath Day is over, people from throughout the region bring their sick and demon-possessed to Jesus for help. Jesus compassionately heals the sick and drives out the demons. Mark uses this text to make sure the reader understands that Jesus' work is not isolated to one or two incidents but that He commanded absolute power over sickness and the demonic realm.

Mark 1:32: The people waited until the sun went down so that it would no longer be the Sabbath Day. Sabbath law had become very explicit by the first century. The rabbinical tradition had enumerated hundreds of laws regarding what constitutes work in violation of their Sabbath law. Even tying or untying a knot was considered a desecration of the Sabbath. Even today, Jews are not permitted to enter an elevator on the Sabbath for fear it might set off a spark. A spark is a fire that is prohibited on the Sabbath. The following verse was used to greatly restrict travel on the Sabbath:

Bear in mind that the Lord has given you the Sabbath; that is why on the sixth day he gives you bread for two days. Everyone is to stay where they are on the seventh day; no one is to go out. (Exodus 16:29, NIV®)

Jewish religious leaders eventually interpreted this verse to mean that no one could travel more than 2,000 cubits or about half a mile. However, various other laws were construed to get around such restrictions such as putting a lunch half a mile from your home the day before. Once you went as far as the normal Sabbath travel law allowed you could stop, make your *home* where your lunch was found, and then travel another half-mile. Jesus specifically refuted such ridiculous traditions that contradicted spirit of the Law if not the letter of the Law. The people in Capernaum observed the tradition they had been taught and waited until evening, *"That evening after sunset"* (Mark 1:32, NIV®), to travel to Jesus. Their zeal was evident in that they brought *"all the sick and demon-possessed."* (Mark 1:32, NIV®).

Mark 1:33: Imagine the sight as Jesus went to the door of Simon's house and saw the crowd of people with sick and deranged men, women, and children. All of these came with a dream that somehow Jesus could heal them. To be sure, Jesus could and did heal their sick. But His main purpose was to bring spiritual healing and wholeness through the gospel (Mark 1:14-

15). The miracles were always intended to authenticate His message rather than propel Jesus to the throne.

Mark 1:34: Jesus healed all kinds of diseases (*"who had various diseases"*) that were brought to Him. The demon-possessed were freed from the spiritual bondage of Satan. Jesus exercised power that was absolute over these things. The demons tried to speak and reveal His identity to the crowd, attempting somehow to damage His mission. Jesus would not even permit them to speak, just to leave. And the demons had to obey because their Creator gave them no such liberty.

Here we see no limit to the power or authority of Jesus. He is a mighty servant of God who crushes the demons and cures the diseased. When troubles plague your life and ministry, remember the power of Jesus. He is able to overcome all evil forces. Your strength rests on the power of Jesus Christ our LORD, not on your own will power or determination.

Jesus' popularity grew exponentially, as the reality of His limitless power became obvious. Were this trend to continue, the town of Capernaum would have moved to crown Him King by force. This was not God's plan. Jesus will have to make a choice to ride the wave of popularity or continue to follow God's plan.

B. Traveling Through Galilee (Mark 1:35-2:12).

(1) Jesus proclaims the purpose of His ministry (Mark 1:35-39).

> ^{35} *Very early in the morning, while it was still dark, Jesus got up, left the house and went off to a solitary place, where he prayed.* ^{36} *Simon and his companions went to look for him,* ^{37} *and when they found him, they exclaimed: "Everyone is looking for you!"* ^{38} *Jesus replied, "Let us go somewhere else—to the nearby villages—so I can preach there also. That is why I have come."* ^{39} *So he traveled throughout Galilee, preaching in their synagogues and driving out demons. (Mark 1:35-39, NIV®)*

The next day, Jesus arose early to find a quiet place to pray. He must determine the Father's will so He can complete His mission. The disciples tracked Him down to let Him know that everyone was searching for Him. But Jesus concluded the Father's will was to preach the gospel to the other towns also. So Jesus traveled through Galilee both preaching the word of God and casting out demons to confirm His authority.

Parallel Passages: Luke 4:42-44

Mark 1:35: Jesus arose while it was still dark to pray. His life consisted of selfless, sacrificial service to others. Such service is an emotional and physical drain. Jesus had encountered

 Insight Bible Commentary Series

countless sick and demon-possessed individuals who each required His personal touch. Jesus needed rest. But He also needed restoration and power for a new day of challenges. Jesus chose to shorten His sleep to spend time in quiet devotion with God the Father. You and I will find power for living to the extent we balance our time of service and time of quiet devotion with the LORD. You cannot hope to accomplish great things for God on your feet without first accomplishing great things with God on your knees.

Mark 1:36-37: Simon and the others went on a serious search for Jesus. They did not know where He had gone because the words *"look for Him"* are from the Greek word *katadioko* meaning to track and hunt down something. Many people were insistently seeking Jesus at Simon's house. Simon had no answer for them. So Simon told Jesus they were looking for Him as if Jesus did not know that already. He performed many miracles the night before. Now the many people wanted more. They were seeking Jesus, the Miracle Worker, not Jesus, the Son of God. Oh that all men would indeed seek the true Jesus for who He is and not just for what He does!

Mark 1:38-39: The prayer of Jesus had a two-fold purpose, as it always should for the believer. First, He had to discern the

Father's will. He needed to understand when to stay and when to go. Second, He had to turn away from anything less than the good and perfect will of the Father. As Paul wrote in Romans:

> *¹ Therefore, I urge you, brothers and sisters, in view of God's mercy, to offer your bodies as a living sacrifice, holy and pleasing to God—this is your true and proper worship. ² Do not conform to the pattern of this world, but be transformed by the renewing of your mind. Then you will be able to test and approve what God's will is—his good, pleasing and perfect will. (Romans 12:1-2, NIV®)*

This is exactly what Jesus was doing early in the morning. He had to face His growing popularity in light of the Father's will to proclaim the good news of the kingdom to all Israel. Jesus faced and overcame the temptation to accept accolades from the people of Capernaum. God the Father had in mind that He preach to the other towns. Leaving was not a popular decision but the right decision for Jesus.

As believers in Christ, we often face such a dilemma. Certain activities can make you extremely popular such as fellowships or personal visits. Certain other activities, such as declaring the whole counsel of God with your life and your lips or confronting a fellow believer in love about a sinful activity can make you extremely unpopular. Through this account in the life of Jesus Christ, we see the real value of prayer. It is necessary to commune with the LORD of all through prayer. We need time to fellowship with Him and receive His special love for us. We need to be in His presence to be changed into the image of Christ (Rom. 8:29). We need to know and acknowledge His will for our lives, committing to do what He has called us to do. As Jesus prayed: *"Here I am, I have come to do your will."* (Hebrews 10:9, NIV®)

Jesus established His own time frame for prayer, even though all that was available to Him was to interrupt His sleep. Sleep is important. Nevertheless, there are times that even sleep must take second place to prayer. Jesus also models for us the power of purpose. He understood His purpose on Earth and all His activity then centered on accomplishing that purpose. Dr. Howard Hendricks, professor at Dallas Theological Seminary, makes this point about Jesus: *"There is considerable power and peace in knowing who you are, where you have come from, and where you are going."*[11] If you want your life to make a difference, make sure you understand these three things. Your life does count to God. It will be maximized the sooner you

---

[11] Hendricks, Howard Dr., Lecture at Dallas Theological Seminary. Source document unknown.

understand your purpose and begin prioritizing your time and activity accordingly.

(2) Jesus heals a leper (Mark 1:40-45).

> ^{40} A man with leprosy came to him and begged him on his knees, "If you are willing, you can make me clean." ^{41} Jesus was indignant. He reached out his hand and touched the man. "I am willing," he said. "Be clean!" ^{42} Immediately the leprosy left him and he was cleansed. ^{43} Jesus sent him away at once with a strong warning: ^{44} "See that you don't tell this to anyone. But go, show yourself to the priest and offer the sacrifices that Moses commanded for your cleansing, as a testimony to them." ^{45} Instead he went out and began to talk freely, spreading the news. As a result, Jesus could no longer enter a town openly but stayed outside in lonely places. Yet the people still came to him from everywhere. (Mark 1:40-45, NIV®)

When approached by a humble leper seeking to be healed, Jesus mercifully healed his leprosy. Jesus gave the man a direct command not to tell anyone but the priest. Instead, the man went all about telling people how Jesus had healed him. Therefore, Jesus could no longer preach in the city. He was forced to stay in the desert places. Yet, people still came to Him from throughout the region.

Mark 1:40: Note how the leper approached our LORD:

- He came to Jesus, indicating his confidence in Jesus' power to heal.

- He *"begged"* Jesus, a word meaning "to call to one's side" or "to call to one's aid." His was a passionate plea to be healed.

- He kneeled down before Jesus, indicating his humility before our LORD.

- He said, *"If you are willing, you can heal me..."* (paraphrased), indicating he knew Jesus had the power but was unsure of His mercy.

The uncertainty about Jesus' mercy seems to be one part of the leper's spiritual need. *"Is God merciful?"* is a question still on the minds of people today, especially when tragedy strikes a family member. On this point, Scripture abounds with affirmation that God is indeed merciful (Num. 14:18; Deut. 4:31, 5:10, 7:9, 32:43; 2 Sam. 24:14; 1 Kings 8:23; 1 Chron. 16:34; Neh 9:17; Psalm 5:7, 13:5, 25:6, 32:10, 57:10, 69:16, 86:15, 89:14, 100:5, 136:1-26, 145:8,147:11; Isa. 30:18, 54:10; 2 Cor. 1:3; Titus 3:5; Heb. 4:16, 8:12; James 5:11; 1 Pet. 1:3; Jude 1:21). Here the very words of the LORD as He revealed His glory to Moses:

> [6] *And he passed in front of Moses, proclaiming, "The Lord, the Lord, the compassionate and gracious God, slow to anger, abounding in love and faithfulness,* [7] *maintaining love to thousands,*

and forgiving wickedness, rebellion and sin. Yet he does not leave the guilty unpunished; he punishes the children and their children for the sin of the parents to the third and fourth generation." (Exodus 34:6-7, NIV®)

From the beginning, God showed mercy to individuals including Lot (Gen. 19:16), Abraham's servant (Gen. 24:27), Jacob (Gen. 32:10-11), Joseph (Gen. 39:21), David (2 Sam. 7:15), Daniel and his friends (Dan. 2:17-18) and countless others (Exo. 20:6; Isa. 55:7). God was also merciful to nations and city-states including Israel (Exo. 15:13; Ezra 3:11; Isa. 14:1), the northern kingdom of Israel (Jer. 31:20), Nineveh of Assyria (Jonah 3:10, 4:11), Athens (Acts 18:22-34), and all Gentile nations (Rom. 9:24-26, 15:9). So if God is merciful by nature, merciful to nations and individuals, then every single person can count on the mercy of God in his or her own life.

But because of his great love for us, God, who is rich in mercy... (Eph. 2:4, NIV®)

Mark 1:41-42: Because He is fully God in nature, Jesus was and is merciful. The 2011 NIV text says that Jesus was *"indignant."* (Mark 1:41, NIV®) This seems a rather strange reaction from Jesus for a man suffering from leprosy. Previous versions of the NIV rendered this word *"filled with compassion."* The Greek word *splagcnisqeiV* indicates He was deeply moved within,

 Insight Bible Commentary Series

literally to have the bowels yearn in sympathy and pity. Jesus really cared for this poor leper who had no hope. So for God in the flesh who is rich in mercy, it makes sense that He would be filled with compassion for the leper. On the other hand, it also makes sense that He would be indignant at the leper questioning if He was willing to extend mercy.

According to the Bible, our LORD is always moved with compassion for those who seek His help. In fact, we are commanded to approach God with boldness when we need help: *"Let us then approach God's throne of grace with confidence, so that we may receive mercy and find grace to help us in our time of need."* (Heb. 4:16, NIV®) God's help reaches down from Heaven to touch the individual at his point of need. True compassion always (1) touches the life of another and (2) actively works to make a difference.

Jesus literally touched the leper. Understand that the Law given to Israel forbids one from touching a leper lest one become defiled by the disease. Lepers were thus considered *unclean* to the Jews (reference Leviticus chapters 13-14). Lepers could not enter the Temple area to worship God. They were to live outside the camp, isolated from the community (Lev. 13:46). If anyone came nearby the leper was to shout *"unclean, unclean!"* (Lev.

13:45, NIV®) While this law obviously had community health in view, the result was great sorrow for the leper. No more could the leper experience a hug, a kiss, or even a pat on the back. His family and friends could not come near. The leper became isolated, alone, and in great pain physically, emotionally, and spiritually. Death was the only hope for relief but even that carried great fear for the leper. The common notion of that day was that such sickness was a direct result of sin in one's life (John 9:2). When Jesus touched this man, He made a tremendous impact on the leper. Jesus demonstrated how great His love was for one whom all others considered defiled and unworthy.

The touch of Jesus came not only with compassion but with great power. Jesus said, *"Be clean"* (v. 41) and the Bible says, *"Immediately the leprosy left him."* (v. 42) The word of God spoken by Jesus came with the power to heal this leper to the uttermost. The skin that was most likely falling from the man's bones was now clear and whole. Jesus completely transformed His body from disease-riddled to disease-ridden.

Jesus still touches lives today. Sometimes He touches those who cry out to Him with immediate physical healing. Sometimes He frees the drug-addict from dependence on mind-altering substances. Sometimes He makes supernatural provision that instantly changes your life. Then again, sometimes He

changes you in ways that are not physically apparent but just as dramatic. The Bible tells us that, *"No one who is born of God will continue to sin, because God's seed remains in them; they cannot go on sinning, because they have been born of God."* (1 John 3:9, NIV®) When you come to Christ for salvation, He changes you inside forever. You become a new creation: *"Therefore, if anyone is in Christ, the new creation has come: The old has gone, the new is here!"* (2 Cor. 5:17, NIV®). The beautiful part is that Jesus continues to change you throughout your life: *"being confident of this, that he who began a good work in you will carry it on to completion until the day of Christ Jesus."* (Phil. 1:6, NIV®)

If you seek His help, Jesus will touch and transform your life. There may be instant changes, such as happened to the leper. Then again, you may not notice the changes because they are primarily spiritual. Spiritual transformation is no less dramatic than physical healing and, over time, will become apparent to you and to others. There is a wonderful story of how the Mt. Rushmore monument came to be. The architect was asked how he could carve such impressive sculptures of the four former presidents. *"Oh, the faces were there all along,"* he said, *"I just had to dynamite away thousands of tons of granite to reveal them!"* Jesus may have to make many changes in your life so that the beautiful new creation He has made in you will appear. But that is OK -- by His work you will daily *"be conformed to the image of his Son."* (Rom. 8:29, NIV®)

Mark 1:43-44: Jesus specifically instructed the leper to tell no one about his miraculous healing. How unfair this seems! You would think Jesus would have wanted the man to tell the whole world about the power of God at work in this teacher named Jesus. Surely this would help spread the good news about Jesus, would it not? But Jesus was not interested in being popularized as a magic healer. He came *"to proclaim good news to the poor."* (Luke 4:18, NIV®) Miracles confirmed to the crowds the authority of His words but were not the focus of His ministry. His instructions seemed unmerciful to the man but, in fact, were an act of mercy to the crowds of people who needed to hear the good news of the kingdom of God. Jesus kept to the heart of His mission that would result in the greatest good.

Also, this leper was still living under the Law given to Israel. There was a provision under the Law for a leper, who had been cured, to be examined by the priest and officially declared cured. Jesus wanted the leper to be obedient to the Law *"as a testimony to them."* (Mark 1:44, NIV®) Imagine the shock in the priest's eyes as he saw the leper was completely healed! The results, however, were undeniable.

Mark 1:45: Instead of following Jesus' command, the leper went everywhere telling people what our LORD had done for him. What the leper did in understandable exuberance made it impossible for Jesus to even go into the city, much less preach the gospel. Everyone wanted to see the miracle worker do more of His *magic* – at least that is how many viewed His miracles.

Two things we need to keep in mind here. First, God does not need our help, however well intentioned, to accomplish His plans. It is always best to do His will, His way, and in His time. When we try to help God out and push things along in our ministry, the same disasters befall us as befell Jesus when the leper disobeyed His command. God's intended ministry is hindered. Jesus had to preach in the desert places because the city became an uproar whenever He tried to preach there. Fewer people heard God's word because the people had to travel out to the desert. Secondly, ministry must have the proclamation of God's word as its preeminent purpose and priority. The excitement of miraculous works will draw many people into the church initially. Such a crowd must continually be fed more and more excitement to stay engaged. When the excitement wears off, people leave. What will always remain a constant is the preaching and teaching of God's word. You cannot sustain a miraculous, entertaining ministry. But you can sustain a ministry that faithfully, accurately, and relevantly teaches the word of God. Believers will feed on the great truths of God's word and grow stronger in faith. *"Consequently, faith comes from hearing the message, and the message is heard through the word about Christ."* (Rom. 10:17, NIV®) Unbelievers also will repent at the preaching of God's word, believe the good news, and enter into the kingdom of God:

> *^{24} But if an unbeliever or an inquirer comes in while everyone is prophesying, they are convicted of sin and are brought under judgment by all, ^{25} as the secrets of their hearts are laid bare. So they will fall down and worship God, exclaiming, "God is really among you!" (1 Cor. 14:24-25, NIV®)*

The shortcoming of the leper was understandable and forgivable. He had experienced the explosive joy of Jesus, His Savior. He was still learning the part about Jesus being LORD. While the Bible does not say specifically, I suspect the leper became a devoted follower of Jesus since He was so quick to testify to Jesus' mighty work in His life. As the Creator of all things, Jesus has incredible power to work in our lives, just as He did with this leper. More importantly, He has incredible compassion that moves Him to use that power according to His perfect will, that which is always best for us.

 Insight Bible Commentary Series

(3) Jesus forgives the sins of a lame man (Mark 2:1-12).

After a long trip of preaching in the desert regions around Galilee, Jesus returns to Capernaum. When the town finds out He is there, they crowd into and around the house where He stayed. Jesus preached the word to the crowd that had gathered there. Several friends of a lame man brought him to Jesus for healing. Unable to get through the crowd, they resort to climbing on the roof of the house, digging a hole through the roof, and lowering the cripple to Jesus. Jesus sees the faith of these friends and grants forgiveness to the lame man. When the scribes privately object to Jesus' apparent blasphemy, Jesus responds by publicly healing the cripple. He states publicly the reason: to demonstrate His authority to forgive sins. The amazed crowd glorified God for such an amazing work.

Parallel passages: Matthew 9:1-8; Luke 5:17-26

a. *Jesus enters Capernaum (Mark 2:1-2).*

> *[1] A few days later, when Jesus again entered Capernaum, the people heard that he had come home. [2] They gathered in such large numbers that there was no room left, not even outside the door, and he preached the word to them. (Mark 2:1-2, NIV®)*

Mark 2:1: Capernaum was the home of Simon peter and Andrew. Jesus and the disciples again return there for rest and refreshment after a long circuit ("*A few days later*") through desert areas to preach. He was not there long before word got out that Jesus was back in town. In fact, Mark records that as soon as the word of Jesus' arrival got out, a crowd gathered.[12] It was the famous evangelist D.L. Moody who once remarked, "*When Christ is in your home, people are going to know about it.*" The people of that town were excited to see and hear Jesus. Here was a man who spoke like no other, treated every person with dignity and godly love, and easily performed miracle upon miracle.

While you and I cannot perform miracles of physical healing like Jesus, we can speak healing words of truth, hope, and love. "*Do your best to present yourself to God as one approved, a worker who does not need to be ashamed and who correctly handles the word of truth.*" (2 Tim. 2:15, NIV®) If you practice this study and assimilation of God's word, you will be able to make relevant application of God's truth to the issues of life. The words you speak and how you say them to people can bring them to the height of joy or to the depths of despair. As the

---

[12] *In Mark 2:2, the Greek word,* euqewV, *is translated "immediately" in the New King James Version but left out of the NIV translation.*

 Insight Bible Commentary Series

Bible says, *"The tongue has the power of life and death, and those who love it will eat its fruit."* (Proverbs 18:21, NIV®) Words do not kill or impart life literally but they do have a dramatic impact. Your words can encourage, comfort, inspire, and persuade when *"Let your conversation be always full of grace, seasoned with salt, so that you may know how to answer everyone."* (Col. 4:6, NIV®) With the same tongue, you can criticize, hate, condemn, and dominate others. As our brother James put it, *"Out of the same mouth come praise and cursing. My brothers and sisters, this should not be."* (James 3:10, NIV®) We need to follow Jesus' example in relating to people who desperately need to hear words of hope and love. Such ministry will attract people with minds and hearts open to the gospel of Jesus Christ.

Mark 2:2: A great crowd gathered as soon as they heard Jesus was there. The text says there was no room at all inside the house and more were outside, longing to get close enough to at least hear what Jesus said. The houses were much smaller then, even for a family with a successful fishing business. Yet people gathered to overflowing to hear Jesus. You see, it really does not matter how big or small or fancy your meeting space is if you are faithful in proclaiming both the love and message of Jesus Christ. People with hearts open to God care less about the aesthetics than the substance and quality of what is proclaimed. Large, beautiful church buildings are truly a blessing to God's people. Just be careful your mission focus is not on building facilities to attract people. It is always the love and the truth that God will honor. Consider the words of Christ in this regard: "Whoever serves me must follow me; and where I am, my servant also will be. My Father will honor the one who serves me." (John 12:26, NIV®) Be sure Christ at the center of your home, your work, and your ministry. For He also said, *"And I, when I am lifted up from the earth, will draw all people to myself."* (John 12:32, NIV®) Proclaiming the LORD Jesus Christ crucified, risen, and coming again will be blessed by God.

Consider the importance of the moment and the sacrifice required. Jesus was very tired after a long journey. A huge crowd gathered to see and hear Jesus. No doubt many wanted only the thrill of seeing Jesus do something amazing. But many also wanted to hear what Jesus had to say. No matter the motivation, Jesus knew their great need was to hear the truth of God's word. This is still a great need for every soul. When a crowd gathers to hear a word from the LORD, you and I must be faithful ministers of the word of God by not wasting any such opportunity. Be prepared to speak. *"The Spirit clearly says that*

in later times some will abandon the faith and follow deceiving spirits and things taught by demons." (1 Tim. 4:1, NIV®) And:

> ³ For the time will come when people will not put up with sound doctrine. Instead, to suit their own desires, they will gather around them a great number of teachers to say what their itching ears want to hear. ⁴ They will turn their ears away from the truth and turn aside to myths. (2 Tim. 4:3-4, NIV®)

Jesus told us to be prepared to sacrifice as He did: "*As long as it is day, we must do the works of him who sent me. Night is coming, when no one can work.*" (John 9:4, NIV®). To minister the word of God to people requires preparation, practice, and preaching -- to "*Always be prepared to give an answer to everyone who asks you to give the reason for the hope that you have. But do this with gentleness and respect.*" (1 Pet. 3:15b, NIV®).

b.   *A lame man's friends bring him to Jesus (Mark 2:3-4).*

> ³ *Some men came, bringing to him a paralyzed man, carried by four of them. ⁴ Since they could not get him to Jesus because of the crowd, they made an opening in the roof above Jesus by digging through it and then lowered the mat the man was lying on. (Mark 2:3-4, NIV®)*

Mark 2:3: A group of people brought with them a special friend who was crippled. The word translated *"paralyzed"* is in a verb tense indicating the man was not born this way but something had happened to cause it -- perhaps an accident or illness at some point in his life. While he was *"carried by four of them,"* the text uses *"them"* for the whole group that came with him, suggesting there were more than four. This particular crippled man had many friends. More importantly, he had many committed friends. They really loved him.

The intent of this group was to bring the crippled man to Jesus for His healing touch. They loved their crippled friend enough to bear his burden by carrying him around. Here is a model for your own life. Take a moment to evaluate your friendships. Are you willing to step in and bear the burden of another? Are you willing to get involved? Will you sweat and labor if needed to help your friend? Are you willing to stop and really listen to your friend? These unnamed people are forever inscribed in Christendom for their great love.

Mark 2:4: Why were the friends of the crippled man unable to bring him to Jesus? The crowd around Jesus both inside and outside the home was too selfish to move aside. They had previously seen Jesus heal everyone who was brought near our LORD. This refusal is a clear indication of how hard their hearts

 Insight Bible Commentary Series

had become. They crowded near to see Jesus perform miracles and hear His amazing words. Yet their love was so cold they would not make room for an obviously crippled man who needed healing. "Why," they may have reasoned in their hearts, "if I move I may lose my place!" This should give each of us pause to ask: Am I passing by people in need on my way to church-related functions? Am I ignoring people because I am too wrapped up in ministry work? Let us make sure our hearts are on fire for true Christian ministry: ministry to people not programs.

Fortunately, the story does not end here. The friends of the crippled man demonstrated the breadth and depth of their love by going beyond what was practical. They were intent on bringing this friend of theirs to Jesus. They climbed up on the roof of the house and dug a large hole through the roof. The typical house in this time had a flat roof with a small railing all the way around it. Often they adjoined other houses. The roof area was used for both private times of meditation and worship as well as public parties. The roof was accessible by an outside stairway. The owners of this house were most likely Simon and Andrew, undoubtedly perturbed with this unrequested remodeling effort. But Simon and Andrew knew Jesus so I am sure they did not raise a strong objection. The text itself does not note any objections. The roof was formed of a concrete-like substance of clay and straw, strong enough to hold the weight of many people. The hole they dug had to be large enough to let down the crippled man on his mat. Creating the hole took some hard work and made quite a mess for the people below. None of that mattered to these faithful friends. They had to bring the crippled man to Jesus.

Here is a model, not only for friendship, but for evangelism. We must be bold in our witness by going beyond what is practical or pragmatic to bring friends and loved ones to Jesus. There will always be obstacles in your soul-winning path. The time may never seem right. The situation may hinder you from getting there the way you want to go. The selfishness of other people may get in the way of your efforts. Do not stop there! Take the example of these faithful friends to heart. Be creative. Think outside the box (or the house as it were). Your goal in evangelism is to bring the word of God to people who may not want to hear it or may not think they want or need it. You should also make it a goal to bring people to the word of God, sort of a push-pull strategy for evangelism. The point is to use every means available to preach the gospel to every person. That is where the true healing begins.

 Insight Bible Commentary Series

c. *Jesus forgives the lame man's sins and Pharisees are indignant (Mark 2:5-7).*

> ⁵ *When Jesus saw their faith, he said to the paralyzed man, "Son, your sins are forgiven."* ⁶ *Now some teachers of the law were sitting there, thinking to themselves,* ⁷ *"Why does this fellow talk like that? He's blaspheming! Who can forgive sins but God alone?" (Mark 2:5-7, NIV®)*

It is a peculiar twist of events at this point. Jesus gives to the cripple what he really needed but was not expecting: forgiveness. The scribes accuse Jesus of doing what only God can do: forgive sins. Their anger is right but for the wrong reason.

Mark 2:5: Jesus *"saw their faith"* the faith of the friends who brought the cripple to Jesus. Whether the cripple had faith in Jesus is not indicated. Jesus did not see the cripple do anything but sit on his bed. But what Jesus saw was a group of people who were desperate to bring their crippled friend to the One person they knew could help and heal. It is the object of one's faith that makes the real difference in your life. Some people speak of having "great" faith or "little" faith. Certainly some people do trust in Jesus more than others. Keep in mind, though, that it is never your faith itself that changes anything. It is the object of your faith, the One in whom you trust. These friends may not have known all there was to know about Jesus but they were confident in His power, wisdom, and mercy. Jesus, also knowing their hearts, saw their faith. He also saw all the ceiling chips He had to dodge as the roof was opened!

Jesus saw the crippled man also. He gave this man the greatest gift anyone could ever receive: the gift of complete forgiveness. There is no thought that the man had sinned to cause his paralysis. The cripple needed forgiveness more than anything. The ability to walk was insignificant compared to his need for cleansing and purity before God. One wonders what his reaction was to being forgiven by Jesus. Was he disappointed or angry? Mark's account does not give us this insight. What we do know is that the man was forgiven of his sins because Jesus declared it so.

Mark 2:6-7: Some of the scribes sitting there immediately had angry thoughts about Jesus' declaration of forgiveness. The scribes were men who were trained in writing (1 Chron. 24:6; Jer. 36:26; Ezra 4:8; Esther 3:12). As keepers of the Law of Moses, the scribes gradually matured from copyists to teachers of the Law (Ezra 7:6 compared to 7:10; also Neh. 8:1-3, 7-8). Interestingly, not all the scribes became indignant. Perhaps they were already persuaded by the utter truth and authority of His preaching, along with the affirming miracles.

 Insight Bible Commentary Series

Certain scribes, though, made a right judgment with a wrong assumption. The word *"thinking"* translates the Greek word "dalogizomai" meaning "to bring together different reasons and reckon them up...used in the NT ... chiefly of thoughts and considerations which are more or less objectionable."[13] It would be utter blasphemy for a mere man to forgive sins. Some so-called churches make it a practice for their religious leaders to *"forgive sins"* on behalf of God. The Bible makes it plain that *"For there is one God and one mediator between God and mankind, the man Christ Jesus."* (1 Tim. 2:5, NIV®) Sin is first and foremost an offense against a holy God. Sin hurts many innocent people also. But God is the One offended by the sin of mankind. Consider that the greater one's character the greater one's offense. Stealing from another thief is not anywhere near as offensive as stealing from an elderly, godly woman. When you magnify this comparison by the absolute holiness, righteousness, and goodness of God, even one sin is an infinite offense. An infinite offense can only carry eternal punishment as a just sentence. For this reason every human being deserves eternal Hell because even one sin requires Hell as a just punishment. How many human beings have sinned only once? *"There is no difference between Jew and Gentile, 23 for all have*

---

[13] *Vine, W.E., Unger, Merrill F., White, Jr., William. Vine's Expository Dictionary of Biblical Words. Thomas Nelson Publishers: Nashville, TN. Copyright 1985. P. 509.*

sinned and fall short of the glory of God." (Rom. 3:22b-23, NIV®) God is the One greatly offended by sin and only God can offer forgiveness. The scribes were correct in their reasoning thus far.

Jesus was a man (a perfect, sinless man, ref. 2 Cor. 5:21). The scribes could see that also. The only problem in their reasoning is that they refused to believe Jesus was more than just a man. They could not refute the truth He proclaimed. Indeed, of all people they would be able to verify from the Old Testament Scripture they knew so well that Jesus was teaching everything in accord with what God had already spoken. They also could not rightly accuse Jesus of sin. Neither could they could deny the miracles He performed before their very eyes. The scribes could not help but consider whether Jesus might be the Christ, the promised Messiah. One cannot help but sympathize, to some degree, with their unbelief since Jesus was there in the flesh before them. The scribes, however, were witnesses to One who was obviously so much more than a mere man. Were they to open their hearts to this possibility, these doubting scribes could have become disciples of Christ themselves.

Today we need to be alert when people under-spiritualize Jesus. Yes, He was a man, a flesh-and-blood human being just like us. The incarnation of God is a wonderful, remarkable fact

of God's compassion in meeting us right where we are, to speak with us face-to-face. Never forget that Jesus was completely human, able to feel the full range of emotions, the victories, the disappointments, the weariness, and even the monotonies of life. Never forget that Jesus is also completely divine. Jesus never stopped being God the Son, second person of the holy Triune God. The universe did not cease to be held together (Heb. 1:3) when Jesus was born that first Christmas night. Make no mistake about His total humanity and total deity.

d. *Jesus heals the lame man to prove His authority to forgive sins (Mark 2:8-12).*

> ^{8} *Immediately Jesus knew in his spirit that this was what they were thinking in their hearts, and he said to them, "Why are you thinking these things? ^{9} Which is easier: to say to this paralyzed man, 'Your sins are forgiven,' or to say, 'Get up, take your mat and walk'? ^{10} But I want you to know that the Son of Man has authority on earth to forgive sins." So he said to the man, ^{11} "I tell you, get up, take your mat and go home." ^{12} He got up, took his mat and walked out in full view of them all. This amazed everyone and they praised God, saying, "We have never seen anything like this!" (Mark 2:8-12, NIV®)*

Jesus knows your heart, your very thoughts in your inmost being (Psalm 139:2-4; Mark 2:8; John 2:25, 6:64). He knew that some of the scribes were objecting to His declaration of forgiveness. In mercy, Jesus provided proof to them that He had this authority. Jesus told them He would heal the cripple so they would know He could also forgive sins. Apparently, it worked. After hearing Him give the purpose for it and then healing the cripple, the people glorified God, as well they and we should.

Mark 2:8: Again, Mark emphasizes the perception of Jesus by using the word *"immediately."* Jesus knew the thoughts of the scribes instantly. In fact, in His divine nature, Jesus knew their thoughts before they thought them. As the Psalmist wrote:

> *² You know when I sit and when I rise; you perceive my thoughts from afar. ³ You discern my going out and my lying down; you are familiar with all my ways. ⁴ Before a word is on my tongue you, Lord, know it completely. (Psalm 139:2-4, NIV®)*

Jesus knows your thoughts because He knows everything. Moreover, Jesus cares what you think. The Bible tells us that, *"⁴ The weapons we fight with are not the weapons of the world. On the contrary, they have divine power to demolish strongholds. ⁵ We demolish arguments and every pretension that sets itself up against the knowledge of God, and we take captive every thought to make it obedient to Christ."* (2 Cor. 10:4-5, NIV®) In this

 Insight Bible Commentary Series

situation, Jesus immediately perceives their thoughts and takes action to correct their faulty reasoning.

Mark 2:9: It is (and always will be) beyond all human knowledge and power to heal instantly. God has mercifully provided man the ability to harness resources from the Earth to create therapeutic medicines, vitamins, and minerals. The Balm of Gilead, for example, was an aromatic resin that had certain medicinal uses in ancient times (Gen. 37:25; Ezekiel 27:17). Make no mistake at this point. Doctors and medicines do not have innate power to heal. Only God possesses that power. Doctors can administer the same drug to two different people. One may be healed and the other may die. So God's act of healing is always an act of mercy. It is God who has declared, *"I will have mercy on whom I have mercy, and I will have compassion on whom I have compassion."* (Rom. 9:15, NIV®) God often uses doctors and drugs as instruments of His healing. He also uses the love and compassion of individuals to aid the heading process. Let us be careful, in this age of scientific breakthroughs, to keep an accurate view of man's limited ability and God's unlimited power. *"Nevertheless, I will bring health and healing to it; I will heal my people and will let them enjoy abundant peace and security."* (Jer. 33:6, NIV®)

In light of this fact, Jesus' question is even more impressive for man cannot heal and neither can he forgive sins. Neither one is easier than the other for man alone. Both are impossible. But as Jesus said, *"What is impossible with man is possible with God."* (Luke 18:27, NIV®) Jesus wanted the people to make no mistake about His authority to forgive sins. That authority does not rest upon a miracle alone. The miracle, rather, points out the divine nature of Jesus. For Jesus, one was just as easy to say as the other -- because He is God in the flesh (John 1:1,14).

Jesus asked the question, *"Which is easier -- forgiveness or healing?"* (Mark 2:9, paraphrased by Randy Lariscy). For Almighty God, healing is easy. God created all things from nothing so restoring the man's malfunctioning legs is but a wisp of effort for God. But for God to forgive sins against His utter perfection, His holiness – that was hard. It cost Him the greatest price ever paid: the life of His only begotten Son (John 10:11). As much as we desire it, physical healing is very visible but temporary -- for this life only. Forgiveness, on the other hand, is invisible but everlasting -- for time and eternity. Jesus gave His best gift first. Then He also healed the man to prove His authority to forgive sins, the authority of God.

 Insight Bible Commentary Series

Mark 2:10-11: The purpose of this particular miracle is *"I want you to know."* Jesus would perform a miraculous healing so that you would know He is the *"LORD of glory."* (1 Cor. 2:8, NIV®) The Greek word "eido" translated *"know"* means to gain specific knowledge by observation without any personal relationship or connection. Jesus did not require them to be His disciples to know He had the authority to forgive sins. Jesus gave them a direct demonstration that He has that power. This knowledge was the seed of truth Jesus planted in their minds hoping it would bear the fruit of faith.

Jesus has the *"authority"* or power on Earth to forgive sins. Because He is God Almighty in the flesh, He alone has the power to condemn or to forgive. The act of forgiveness indicated here is the releasing of the crippled man from the penalty of his sins. He did not deserve such grace but it was granted to him anyway. The offense of his sins was canceled completely. Such forgiveness is very hard for human beings to give, even harder to receive. One who is completely forgiven of terrible sins has a strong desire to repay the offended party. Jesus requires no such repayment. His forgiveness is granted freely to all who will believe in Him.

Mark 2:12: Jesus told the cripple to get up and go. He had been bound by whatever affliction caused his legs to fail. Instantly, Jesus restored their strength. The healing occurred *"immediately"* (NKJV) in full view of the crowd. There could be no doubt that Jesus had performed a miracle. The people obviously knew this man had been a complete cripple and now was whole. The reaction was just as immediate: *"This amazed everyone and they praised God."* Jesus was no magician. He truly intervened in the natural processes by healing the man's disease completely. The man who was crippled stood up and walked before their very eyes. Further, Jesus was not attempting to make a name for Himself nor draw attention to His greatness. The purpose was to demonstrate the reality of His divine nature. The people exclaimed, *"We have never seen anything like this!"* The natural man cannot help but glory in himself. When we do something truly wonderful we get hurt if no one notices us. Jesus took no delight in the applause of men but rejoiced in their faith. We should be so humble as He.

As we see in this example of the friends of this crippled man, faith produces faithfulness. The faith itself is not a power. The One in whom that faith is placed, if it is Jesus Christ, has the power to accomplish great things. It is a mystery why and how God works through weak, sin prone individuals. Indeed, He

 Insight Bible Commentary Series

does work in and through individuals that are willing to place their faith in Him.

> ^{27} But God chose the foolish things of the world to shame the wise; God chose the weak things of the world to shame the strong. ^{28} God chose the lowly things of this world and the despised things—and the things that are not—to nullify the things that are, ^{29} so that no one may boast before him." (1 Cor. 1:27-29, NIV®)

Convinced of Jesus' divine nature, power to heal, and unique capacity to forgive sins, we too will bring people to Christ. As we also learn in this account, believers need to work together to bring people to Christ. This is, in fact, our primary task until Jesus returns. An old poem states it so well:

> *Only one life, 'twill soon be past.*
> *Only what's done for Christ will last.*[14]

Determine that you will join together with other believers in faith, working together to bring the gospel to your community. Let nothing hinder your plans and let no obstacle prevent you from bringing your lost friends to Jesus. He alone has the power to heal and forgive.

---

[14] Studd, C.T. Retrieved 7/16/2012 at http://hockleys.org/2009/05/quote-only-one-life-twill-soon-be-past-poem/

C. Encountering Questions (Mark 2:13-3:6).

In this section of Scripture, the scribes and Pharisees begin to seriously question Jesus. They question Jesus' spirituality in social settings, in private devotions, and on the Sabbath day. His methods and teachings were markedly different than their own. He seemed to have little regard for the traditions around the Law of Moses, held in such high regard by the Pharisees. How could a teacher of God's word behave as Jesus did? Jesus' failure to meet their own self-righteous standards became one of the main sources of conflict throughout His earthly ministry. Ultimately, the religious leaders rejected Jesus as Christ because He failed to conform to their own distorted view of how Christ should act and what He should accomplish.

(1) Jesus ministers to publicans and sinners (Mark 2:13-17).

> *[13] Once again Jesus went out beside the lake. A large crowd came to him, and he began to teach them. [14] As he walked along, he saw Levi son of Alphaeus sitting at the tax collector's booth. "Follow me," Jesus told him, and Levi got up and followed him.*
>
> *[15] While Jesus was having dinner at Levi's house, many tax collectors and sinners were eating with*

Insight Bible Commentary Series

him and his disciples, for there were many who followed him. ^{16} When the teachers of the law who were Pharisees saw him eating with the sinners and tax collectors, they asked his disciples: "Why does he eat with tax collectors and sinners?" ^{17} On hearing this, Jesus said to them, "It is not the healthy who need a doctor, but the sick. I have not come to call the righteous, but sinners." (Mark 2:13-17, NIV®)

As He again traveled to the Sea of Galilee teaching the word of God, Jesus called Levi, whom we know as Matthew, to follow Him. Matthew left his work and followed Jesus, even inviting Jesus and all the disciples to a dinner in his home. Matthew's shady friends were there. The religious leaders objected to this supposed prophet who dined with such social outcasts. Jesus emphasized the nature of His mission: to call sinners to repentance. You cannot call sinners to repentance if you only hang out with those who consider themselves *"righteous."* (v. 17)

Parallel passages: Matthew 9:9-13; Luke 5:27-32

Mark 2:13: Jesus and the disciples left Capernaum for another mission trip. The people of that area heard about it and flocked to Him by the Sea of Galilee. Capernaum is on the north-northwest side of the Sea of Galilee just a few miles from where the Jordan River enters. With a large crowd gathered around Him, Jesus again teaches them the word of God. Jesus was always ready to teach. In any congregational setting, never waste a teachable moment. If a large crowd gathers, feed them the word of God as Jesus did.

Mark 2:14: The call of a tax collector named *"Levi the son of Alphaeus"* presents an interesting puzzle to the modern reader. Later, in chapter 3, the twelve disciples are mentioned and Levi does not appear in the list -- but Matthew is there. The gospel of Luke records the call of Levi/Matthew in the same way. In the parallel passage of the tax collector's call, Matthew 9:9-13, the name most familiar to modern readers is used: Matthew. Chapter 10 of Matthew records the twelve disciples, specifically listing Matthew as *"Matthew the tax collector." (Matthew 10:3, NIV®)* So from the gospel of Matthew we know that Matthew is the tax collector, Levi, called by Jesus to be one of the twelve. Why did Mark and Luke refer to him with two different Jewish names? Lane proposes this solution:

> *In Ch. 2:14 Mark is concerned to illustrate the radical character of Jesus' call, and that it is the*

 Insight Bible Commentary Series

nature of the call, rather than the name of the one called, which is of primary importance.[15]

Lane's solution is entirely possible but there is nothing in the gospel accounts of either Mark or Luke to connect Levi with Matthew. Perhaps the readers of Mark's early gospel account were familiar enough with Levi/Matthew that an explanation was considered unnecessary.

Matthew had been sitting *"at the tax collector's booth"* meaning he was a tax collector. Rome established a taxation system that was to be administered by the local governor chosen by Rome, in this case Herod Antipas. A fixed annual fee was paid to Rome via the local governor. Local people were hired as tax collectors most likely because of how well they knew the people and the area. The tax collectors were free to collect as much money as they desired so long as the annual fee was paid. Greed, the obvious consequence of such a system, quickly became the driving force behind extortion of the common citizen's money. As a result, the tax collectors were hated by the Jewish people. Because the tax collectors were Jews working for

---

[15] Lane, William. *The Gospel of Mark: New International Commentary on the New Testament.* Wm. B. Eerdmans Publishing Company: Grand Rapids, Michigan. Copyright 1974. pp. 100-101.

the oppressive Roman government, they were hated even more than the Romans. The Jewish people considered them traitors, rejecting them socially and relationally. As a tax collector, Matthew was among those who were bitterly despised.

Jesus, however, did not despise Matthew though his lifestyle was corrupt and sinful. Jesus loved Matthew, calling him by name to be His disciple. Matthew was called to be a disciple with the same words Jesus used for the other disciples: *"Follow Me!" (Matt. 4:19; John 1:43, NIV®)* His response to Jesus' command is a model of obedience. This is how Jesus calls you to be His disciple today: He calls you by name. The Holy Spirit reaches into your heart with the gospel of Jesus Christ saying, *"Follow Me!"* Like Matthew, our response needs to be immediate.

Note the simplicity of Jesus' command to *"Follow Me!" (Mark 2:14, NIV®)* Jesus is saying, "Just trust Me, watch Me, listen to Me, and do what I do." It requires only the simplest of faith as we see in Matthew's response. More importantly, Jesus is not asking Matthew to memorize and recite a creed. The command is to follow a person - the person of Jesus Christ. Religious creeds and statements of faith are fine for the purpose of unifying a religious organization and declaring that organization's beliefs. But creeds intentionally set one group of

 Insight Bible Commentary Series

people apart from other people. They divide us. And while this may be necessary for an organization, it is not particularly helpful for one's individual spiritual growth. Creeds can be compromised. If we are asked to follow a creed, the first time temptation strikes we think of ways to "bend the rule." You can bend or compromise a creed. But you cannot bend or compromise the person of Jesus.

Jesus made it clear we are to follow Him. Jesus unites people around this common goal: to walk with Him. You follow Him which, by definition, keeps you from changing anything about Him to accommodate your own personal agenda. You will change as you follow Him. Jesus will never change – *"I, the LORD, do not change." (Malachi 3:6, NIV®)*

Mark 2:15-16: Matthew hosted a dinner banquet for all his friends, those of low reputation like Matthew all banding together. It has been said, *"A person is known by the company he keeps."* Matthew was surrounded by "tax collectors," a word referring to those in the business of collecting taxes on behalf of Rome. He was also with "sinners," indicating those who had no regard for the Law, constantly lived in ceremonial uncleanness, and liked it that way. They were what we might call "low-life."

But they were Matthew's friends and they were celebrating with him.

Matthew invited his new friends to the dinner: Jesus and His disciples. His obvious motive was to share Jesus with all of his "low-life" friends. It is noteworthy that Jesus readily attended such an event. His disciples simply followed wherever Jesus went. Their level of comfort with this crowd is not known. But Jesus was eating and drinking with them (2:16).

Jesus invited Matthew's friends to become His friend. He did not require anyone to "clean up his act" or become pious and religious. He offered forgiveness and new life to anyone who would take it. Never did Jesus force Himself on anyone. Jesus took risks in order to reach out in love to people in all walks of life. This is a perfect model for you and I as we work, go to school, shop for groceries, or take a walk through the neighborhood. Never be afraid to befriend someone who needs to know the love and message of Christ. Jesus took advantage of each opportunity with people to demonstrate His perfect love, teach the truth of God, and call people to follow Him.

Jesus did not insulate Himself or His disciples from unbelievers. Families today seem content to cocoon themselves in their own homes with their own entertainment than to

 Insight Bible Commentary Series

socialize with other families. Neighbors live side-by-side for years without even knowing each other's names. The religious community sometimes becomes insulated into its "own kind." If your neighbor is not a Christian, then no social contact is thought to be a good thing. The truly "spiritual" giants only work, play, and go to school with other like-minded people of faith. Jesus shatters this evil notion by joining Matthew's friends. Jesus was more than willing to associate with people of low reputation, even at the expense of His own reputation in the religious community. *"If you love those who love you, what reward will you get? Are not even the tax collectors doing that? And if you greet only your brothers, what are you doing more than others? Do not even pagans do that?" (Matt. 5:46-47, NIV®)* Jesus kept His redemptive mission clearly in focus.

Mark 2:17: Jesus neither avoided the *"sinners"* nor did He ignore the scribes and Pharisees. He heard what they said: *"Why does he eat with tax collectors and sinners?" (Mark 2:16, NIV®)* Jesus answered them plainly: *"It is not the healthy who need a doctor, but the sick. I have not come to call the righteous, but sinners." (Mark 2:17, NIV®)* If you are not sick, you will not go to a doctor for healing. Moreover, if you think you are not sick, you will also avoid the doctor. The scribes and Pharisees thought that their outward obedience to God's law made them whole.

They had no need of repentance and salvation because they decided their good works were good enough for themselves. Had they consulted the word of God *(the very word they were entrusted to teach)* they would have found this startling truth about how sick they really were:

> *The heart is deceitful above all things and beyond cure. Who can understand it? (Jer. 17:9, NIV®)*
>
> *See, he is puffed up; his desires are not upright— but the righteous will live by his faith. (Hab. 2:4, NIV®)*
>
> *The Lord says: "These people come near to me with their mouth and honor me with their lips, but their hearts are far from me. Their worship of me is made up only of rules taught by men. (Isa. 29:13, NIV®)*
>
> *The fool says in his heart, "There is no God." They are corrupt, their deeds are vile; there is no one who does good. The LORD looks down from heaven on the sons of men to see if there are any who understand, any who seek God. All have turned aside, they have together become corrupt; there is no one who does good, not even one. (Psa. 14:1-3, NIV®)*

One cannot become righteous in God's eyes without perfect obedience to the Law. Jesus said, *"Be perfect, therefore, as your heavenly Father is perfect" (Matt. 5:48, KJV)*. This is obvious to God who searches the hearts and minds of people.

Until a person is willing to acknowledge his sin before a holy God, he cannot and will not seek Jesus to heal his spiritual sickness.

Jesus came not to call the righteous, that is, the self-righteous. He came to call sinners to repentance. Repentance is a turning away from self-willed sin and turning instead to God through faith in the LORD Jesus Christ (cf. Mark 1:15 notes regarding repentance). If you are willing to approach God in humility, acknowledging your sin and your need to be cleansed of it, Jesus can help you. *"'Come now, let us reason together,' says the LORD. 'Though your sins are like scarlet, they shall be as white as snow; though they are red as crimson, they shall be like wool.'" (Isa. 1:18, NIV®)* It is through faith in Jesus Christ alone *"In whom we have redemption, the forgiveness of sins." (Col. 1:14, NIV®)* Jesus takes you as a sinner and gives you forgiveness of sins, healing your fatal spiritual disease called sin, granting you eternal life instead. This is the marvelous grace of God! Unworthy sinners redeemed and made new by the God who loves you without limit.

(2) Jesus delineates new ways for the new life He offers (Mark 2:18-22).

> [18] *Now John's disciples and the Pharisees were fasting. Some people came and asked Jesus, "How is it that John's disciples and the disciples of the Pharisees are fasting, but yours are not?"* [19] *Jesus answered, "How can the guests of the bridegroom fast while he is with them? They cannot, so long as they have him with them.* [20] *But the time will come when the bridegroom will be taken from them, and on that day they will fast.* [21] *"No one sews a patch of unshrunk cloth on an old garment. Otherwise, the new piece will pull away from the old, making the tear worse.* [22] *And no one pours new wine into old wineskins. Otherwise, the wine will burst the skins, and both the wine and the wineskins will be ruined. No, they pour new wine into new wineskins." (Mark 2:18-22, NIV®)*

The tradition of the day for spirituality was fasting. The Pharisees encouraged fasting twice a week (see Luke 18:12) as evidence of spirituality. Even the disciples of John the Baptist were fasting. Yet Jesus and His disciples were having a feast, not a fast. The tradition of the Pharisees was in conflict with the non-traditional approach of Jesus. Jesus used two analogies to make His point that there is a new covenant being brought forth into the world. This new covenant requires a new way of approaching spirituality -- one that is first concerned with the

internal thoughts and motivations that drive the external behavior.

Parallel passages: Matthew 9:14-17; Luke 5:33-39

Mark 2:18: *"John's disciples"* were disciples of John the Baptist. Apparently, some of those who followed the teachings of John the Baptist gave no heed when he pointed them to Jesus Christ:

> *^{29} The next day John saw Jesus coming toward him and said, "Look, the Lamb of God, who takes away the sin of the world! ^{30} This is the one I meant when I said, 'A man who comes after me has surpassed me because he was before me.' ^{31} I myself did not know him, but the reason I came baptizing with water was that he might be revealed to Israel." (John 1:29-31, NIV®)*

The "Pharisees" were one of the ruling religious groups in Israel, subservient to Roman rule at the time. They approached Jesus with an obvious question about His religious practices – "why don't you conform to our traditions?"

Mark 2:19-20: Fasting is a type of soul-grieving. One fasts by sacrificing one thing, usually food, in order to draw close to the LORD in a time of prayer and communion. The soul of a believer longs for intimacy with the LORD. Many saints for thousands of years have practiced some form of fasting in pursuit of this intimacy.

In these two verses, Jesus asks a question where the obvious answer is "no." In a wedding feast, the bridegroom invites many to celebrate with him the sacred gift of marriage. They cannot fast at a wedding feast; rather, they should be celebrating because the bridegroom is right there with them. But one day, the bride and the bridegroom would leave to begin their own family. The friends of the bridegroom will then long for the intimate time they used to have with the bridegroom.

Our spiritual relationship with the LORD Jesus Christ is similar to the friends of the bridegroom. In your longing to be close to Him, you may fast because He is not physically here with you. Fasting may provide the opportunity for you to set aside things that distract you and allow you to focus in on your relationship with Him. The disciples of Christ at this time had Jesus, the *"bridegroom,"* with them in the flesh. Fasting was unthinkable because they had direct communion with our LORD. After Jesus ascended to the Father in Heaven, there would be times they would fast, longing for the intimacy they once enjoyed with Him face-to-face.

There is another interpretation of this teaching to consider. The time when the *"bridegroom will be taken from them"* could possibly allude to the three days when Jesus was buried after His crucifixion. If the phrase is indicating this time, then there would be no need of fasting today because Jesus has risen from the grave. Those who believe in Him are now indwelt by the Holy Spirit (John 7:37-39), also referred to as the *"Spirit of Jesus." (1 Peter 1:11)* Jesus is with us in an even more intimate way than face-to-face. He dwells with us in the deepest reaches of our soul. Nevertheless, we know from experience that many believers still find fasting to be a profitable spiritual discipline.

Mark 2:21-22: Using two analogies, Jesus makes it clear that things are going to be different. First, He compares the old religious traditions to the present spiritual reality that He has instituted. If one were to sew a patch of unshrunk cloth onto an old shirt, the new cloth would shrink in the first washing and pull itself apart from the old cloth on the shirt. The result would be an unusable shirt. Similarly, no one puts new wine (that is, unfermented wine) into an old wineskin. The old wineskin previously housed wine that fermented. As that process unfolds, gas is released that expands the size of the wineskin. There is some room for expansion in the skins but at some point they will break. Putting new wine into an old wineskin is a sure way to break the skin. The result would again be unusable wine.

To try and continue old religious traditions under the new spiritual reality brought about by His life, death, burial, and resurrection. Later Jesus would speak of this reality as the *"new covenant in My blood." (Luke 22:20, NIV®)* The religious tradition that marked Judaism of that day was going to change. The religious leaders - Pharisees, Sadducees, and teachers of the Law - saw this as blasphemy. But Jesus was merely fulfilling the will of God the Father and, in actuality, fulfilling the very law the religious leaders were supposed to teach (Matthew 5:17).

(3) Jesus defies the Sabbath traditions of men (Mark 2:23-28).

> *[23] One Sabbath Jesus was going through the grainfields, and as his disciples walked along, they began to pick some heads of grain. [24] The Pharisees said to him, "Look, why are they doing what is unlawful on the Sabbath?"[25] He answered, "Have you never read what David did when he and his companions were hungry and in need? [26] In the days of Abiathar the high priest, he entered the house of God and ate the consecrated bread, which is lawful only for priests to eat. And he also gave some to his*

 Insight Bible Commentary Series

companions." ²⁷ Then he said to them, "The Sabbath was made for man, not man for the Sabbath. ²⁸ So the Son of Man is Lord even of the Sabbath." (Mark 2:23-28, NIV®)

As the Pharisees continue to watch and criticize Jesus and His disciples, Jesus provides an important teaching regarding the Sabbath. As the Son of God, Jesus was also the Great High Priest of God to the world (ref. Hebrews 4:14-5:10 for a discussion of this point). Yet the sacrifices and offerings of the people that supported the Levitical priests were not shared with Jesus. He and His disciples lived on the generosity of others. As a result, they were often hungry and in need of basic supplies.

Parallel passages: Matthew 12:1-8; Luke 6:1-5

Mark 2:23-24: The Sabbath was the last day of the week - Sundown on Friday evening to Sundown on Saturday evening by the modern calendar. It was on this day that the Law of Moses commanded, "*8 Remember the Sabbath day by keeping it holy. 9 Six days you shall labor and do all your work, 10 but the seventh day is a sabbath to the Lord your God. On it you shall not do any work...*" *(Exodus 20:8-10, NIV®)* Rabbinical tradition attempted to define work so as to help people keep the Sabbath rest. In so doing, they began to include so many facets of life into the category of *"work"* that it became a huge burden on people to keep. As the disciples "began to pick some heads of grain" - that is, they were pulling the heads of grain off the plants as they walked through the field and, rubbing them between their palms, would eat the meal from the grain.

This was problematic for the Pharisees who saw this act as harvesting grain, grinding, and preparing bread. Hence, they were working on the Sabbath. Their question was actually an accusation of a Sabbath law violation. Since they were looking for any excuse to discredit and condemn Jesus, this seemed to be a clear violation of the Law of Moses.

Mark 2:25-28: Jesus made three points to help the Pharisees understand the futility of their viewpoint:

    i.   **The Priority of Life:** Jesus reminded them (v. 25) of what King David had done in the past regarding eating bread consecrated to the LORD (1 Samuel 21:1-6). As the legitimate king and spiritual leader of Israel, David knew the Law of Moses. At the same time, circumstances were not normal. He had been unjustly chased away by Saul and his army. David and his men were on the run and literally starving. At the time, the consecrated bread was all that was available. The

priest gave it to David and his men. Between a choice to obey a ritual law or to feed starving men, the priority with God is life. The Law is important but people are more important. The Pharisees refused to accept that interpretation.

ii. **The Purpose of the Sabbath:** God gave the Sabbath day of rest to mankind (v. 27) because He knows that we need it. No one can work seven days a week and remain effective. We need rest. So the Sabbath provides a clear cycle for mankind: work six days and rest for one. The Sabbath was made for man's benefit.

The reverse is just not true. In a fallen world, man was not made to perfectly keep a complete day of Sabbath rest. Out of control things happen in a sin-cursed world. And man himself is imperfect in keeping any law, including the Sabbath. The Sabbath was commanded to provide rest and relief for man, not to become a burden. Man certainly cannot make perfect rest for himself, no matter how hard he tries. Ultimately our rest comes through the finished work of Jesus Christ (Heb. 4:3-9).

The attitude and teaching of the Pharisees regarding the Sabbath had become a whip on the backs of people. This was never God's design for the Sabbath. It was intended to be a benefit not a burden.

iii. **The Preeminence of Jesus:** As the *"Son of man" (v. 28)* - a title which Jesus seemed to enjoy using about Himself since it speaks directly of God who became a human being (John 1:1,14) - Jesus had every right to make or break a Sabbath law. But certainly He had the authority to provide correct interpretation of that law. He is *"Lord even of the Sabbath." (v. 28)*

(4) Pharisees begin their plot to kill Jesus (Mark 3:1-6).

¹ Another time Jesus went into the synagogue, and a man with a shriveled hand was there. ² Some of them were looking for a reason to accuse Jesus, so they watched him closely to see if he would heal him on the Sabbath. ³ Jesus said to the man with the shriveled hand, "Stand up in front of everyone." ⁴ Then Jesus asked them, "Which is lawful on the Sabbath: to do good or to do evil, to save life or to kill?" But they remained silent. ⁵

 **Insight Bible Commentary Series**

He looked around at them in anger and, deeply distressed at their stubborn hearts, said to the man, "Stretch out your hand." He stretched it out, and his hand was completely restored. ⁶ Then the Pharisees went out and began to plot with the Herodians how they might kill Jesus. (Mark 3:1-6, NIV®)

As Jesus goes to the synagogue on the Sabbath, the Pharisees are there with a critical, watchful eye. Once again, their Sabbath traditions are in question. They were concerned whether Jesus would heal someone on the Sabbath. A man with a disabled hand was there. Jesus questioned the Pharisees regarding their narrow interpretation of the Sabbath law. Getting no response from them, Jesus heals the man in plain view of the congregation and the Pharisees. Afterward, the Pharisees began to plot to kill Jesus.

Parallel passages: Matthew 12:9-14; Luke 6:6-11

Mark 3:1-2: On the Sabbath, it was the custom of Jesus to go to the local synagogue to worship and to teach. As Jesus is watched by some of the religious leaders, they ponder whether He would heal anyone on the Sabbath. They had seen His miracles on other occasions. Now, since it was the Sabbath and all work was forbidden, they watched to see if Jesus would *"work"* on the Sabbath by healing someone. The question seems absurd to us today. If one had the power to heal, he should use it to heal everyone he could, anytime he could. But in the 1st century the Sabbath command to rest from work had been perverted into miniscule rules and regulations that made the day impossible to observe, much less enjoy. Even though *"the LORD blessed the Sabbath day and made it holy," (Exodus 20:11, NIV®)* the Pharisees used it as a way to control and punish people. They actually equated healing someone with *"work"* that was to be avoided on the Sabbath at all cost.

As we saw in mark 2:23-28, there is a priority on life over ritual law. Just as a man should not be permitted to starve on the Sabbath, a man should not be denied a healing touch either.

Mark 3:3-4: Jesus had the man stand up before the congregation. He gave the Pharisees a chance to acknowledge the righteousness of God in healing on the Sabbath. His question to them seems to have an obvious answer: *"Which is lawful on the Sabbath: to do good or to do evil, to save life or to kill?" (v. 4)* It had nothing to do with healing but provided the greater context for His upcoming miracle. Would the Pharisees acknowledge that good works on the Sabbath were lawful? Would they acknowledge that saving life was lawful? These were no trick questions. And in light of the obvious answer, the

 Insight Bible Commentary Series

Pharisees remained silent. Their hearts were stubbornly set on their own tradition regardless of how foolish or evil it was. The Pharisees could not allow Jesus to be "right" in the eyes of the public for this would diminish their own power and prestige. In the end, their pride was more important than a person in need of medical help.

Mark 3:5: Jesus felt *"anger" (v. 5)* - from the Greek word "orge" meaning a violent passion - toward the Pharisees. Their prideful hearts would no longer acknowledge basic right and wrong. Their thinking and teaching was corrupt. As the religious leaders of the day, Jesus was *"deeply distressed" (v. 5)* over their self-inflicted spiritual emptiness and also because of the number of people they would influence over time. To make His point crystal clear, Jesus healed the man's hand in view of everyone.

Mark 3:6: The public healing in plain view of the Pharisees humiliated them. They left the synagogue and began to plot to kill Jesus. This is the first time the gospel of Mark records the murderous intent of the religious leaders toward Jesus. The "Herodians" were civic leaders, a group of people who supported the local government over Israel that had been set up by the

Romans. Rome generally installed local leadership that had pledged loyalty to Caesar in countries they had conquered.

D. Organizing the Disciples (Mark 3:7-35).

In this passage, Jesus establishes His authority in various areas: in the physical world, in the spiritual world, in His group of disciples, and even in His family. In calling twelve of His specially selected disciples, Jesus names them Apostles and grants them power to heal the sick and drive out demons in His name. His purpose in so doing is not to elevate the disciples but to further spread the good news of the kingdom of God (Mark 1:14-15).

(1) Jesus teaches multitudes from Israel and the surrounding nations. (Mark 3:7-12).

> *⁷ Jesus withdrew with his disciples to the lake, and a large crowd from Galilee followed. ⁸ When they heard about all he was doing, many people came to him from Judea, Jerusalem, Idumea, and the regions across the Jordan and around Tyre and Sidon. ⁹ Because of the crowd he told his disciples to have a small boat ready for him, to keep the people from crowding him. ¹⁰ For he had healed many, so that those with diseases were pushing forward to touch him. ¹¹ Whenever the impure spirits saw him, they fell down before him and cried out, "You are the Son of God." ¹² But he*

 Insight Bible Commentary Series

gave them strict orders not to tell others about him. (Mark 3:7-12, NIV®)

Parallel passages: Matthew 9:35-38

Mark 3:7: After healing a man on the Sabbath and humiliating the Pharisees as a result, Jesus withdrew to the *"lake"* (the Sea of Galilee). His disciples followed Him.

Mark 3:8: *"When they heard all He was doing"* – A large crowd began to gather around Jesus as they had heard of the miracles He was performing. Word had gotten to Tyre and Sidon (this is in modern day Lebanon), Judea and Jerusalem (southern Israel), across the Jordan River (modern day Jordan), and Idumea (an area southeast of the Dead Sea, the land of ancient Edom).

Mark 3:10: *"For He had healed many"* - As the Son of God, Jesus possessed the power of God. According to His perfect will He healed the diseases of many people. These miracles brought even more people to Him, desperate to tough Him and be healed.

Mark 3:11: *"Evil spirits saw Him"* - The *"evil"* or unclean spirits are the fallen angels who followed Lucifer in His rebellion against God (Matthew 25:41; Revelation 12:9). At times they would demonize people who were not in a right relationship with God. Some use the term "demon possession." But possession implies ownership. It is God Himself who owns everything. What we hear called "demon possession" is, in reality, significant influence over the thoughts and actions of a person. One word from the LORD Jesus and these evil spirits had to flee.

Mark 3:12: *"He gave them strict orders not to tell who He was"* - Jesus did not want to be proclaimed the Messiah (Christ) by demons. He wanted people to figure this out for themselves based on His words and His works of God.

(2) Jesus calls out His twelve disciples (Mark 3:13-19).

> *[13] Jesus went up on a mountainside and called to him those he wanted, and they came to him. [14] He appointed twelve that they might be with him and that he might send them out to preach [15] and to have authority to drive out demons. [16] These are the twelve he appointed: Simon (to whom he gave the name Peter), [17] James son of Zebedee and his brother John (to them he gave the name Boanerges, which means "sons of thunder"), [18] Andrew, Philip, Bartholomew, Matthew, Thomas, James son of Alphaeus, Thaddaeus, Simon the Zealot [19] and Judas Iscariot, who betrayed him. (Mark 3:13-19, NIV®)*

Now Jesus calls out twelve specially picked disciples to perform the role of Apostle - a word meaning "one who is sent." These apostles would share the good news of the kingdom with others, thereby multiplying Jesus' ministry.

 Insight Bible Commentary Series

Parallel passages: Matthew 10:1-4; Luke 6:12-15

Mark 3:13-19: After much prayer and consideration, Jesus chose twelve of His disciples to be Apostles. Their main duty was to be with Jesus so they could learn His ways intimately and preach His word accurately. They were given authority to drive out evil spirits in His name. Note that it was *"those He wanted"* – each of the twelve were specially chosen for this role. The twelve He chose were:

Name	Meaning	Insights
Simon Peter	Simon means *flat-nosed*[16] and Peter means *rock*.	Jesus said, *"you are Peter [rock], and on this rock [large rock] I will build My church."* (Matthew 16:18, NIV®) Some take this to mean that Peter would be the rock upon which the church is built and, hence, Peter would head up the church (Roman Catholic tradition). But note the word play - though Peter was a *rock*, the church of Jesus Christ would be built on a *large foundation rock*. The large rock is the foundation stone of the church - Jesus Himself (1 Cor. 3:10-11; Eph. 2:20). Upon the confession that Jesus is the Christ (Mat. 16:16), Jesus used the apostles to build His church.

---

[16] Butler, Trent C. *Holman Bible Dictionary*. Holman Bible Publishers: Nashville, TN. Copyright 1991. p. 1281.

Name	Meaning	Insights
		But make no mistake - Jesus is the foundation (Eph. 3:11) and He will build His church. Peter was a leader in the early church but the church at Jerusalem was led by James, half-brother of Jesus (Acts 15:12-21, esp. v13).
James	It is the English form of *Jacob*.[17]	The name Jacob means *He grasps the heel* - one who reaches beyond what is his to take from another; a deceiver or cheat. He was the son of Zebedee, a fisherman.
John	Means Yahweh has been gracious.[18]	Son of Zebedee, brother of James. He is called the *"disciple whom Jesus loved,"* (John 13:23, 19:26, 21:7, 21:20, NIV®) one of Jesus' closest friends during His earthly ministry.
Andrew	Means manly or warrior	He was the brother of Simon Peter (Matthew 4:18).
Philip	Means friend of horses	He was from the town of Bethsaida (John 1:44), a friend of Nathanael (John 1:45).
Bartholomew	Means ridged or furrow	He was the son of Tolmai.
Matthew	Means the gift of Yahweh[19]	A tax collector Jesus called to *"Follow Me."* (Matthew 4:19, NIV®)
Thomas	Means twin[20]	He is known today as *Doubting Thomas* for his skepticism of

---

[17] *Ibid*. p. 743.
[18] *Ibid*. p. 803.
[19] *Ibid*. p. 932.

 Insight Bible Commentary Series

Name	Meaning	Insights
		Jesus' resurrection (John 20:24-25). He was, however, a brave man, willing to go with Jesus to Jerusalem while facing certain death (John 11:16).
James	Jacobus, variant of Jacob	He was the son of Alphaeus.
Thaddaeus	Means gift of God[21]	Nothing else is mentioned regarding Thaddaeus in Scripture.
Simon the Zealot	Simon means *flat-nosed*	The zealots were a group of Jews who were intent on overthrowing by force the Roman rule of Palestine.
Judas Iscariot	Judas means *Praise Yahweh*.[22] Iscariot means *from Kerioth*.[23]	Kerioth refers to cities in the area of Moab. Judas is, perhaps, the most intriguing choice from an apostle since he would later betray Jesus. Apparently Jesus saw great potential in Judas that He worked hard to develop. Unfortunately, Judas would ultimately reject Jesus' authority and message.

(3) Scribes accuse Jesus of being demon-possessed. (Mark 3:20-30).

[20] Then Jesus entered a house, and again a crowd gathered, so that he and his disciples were not

---

[20] *Ibid. p. 1344.*
[21] *Ibid. p. 1336.*
[22] *Ibid. p. 821.*
[23] *Ibid. p. 837.*

even able to eat. ²¹ When his family heard about this, they went to take charge of him, for they said, "He is out of his mind." ²² And the teachers of the law who came down from Jerusalem said, "He is possessed by Beelzebul! By the prince of demons he is driving out demons." ²³ So Jesus called them over to him and began to speak to them in parables: "How can Satan drive out Satan? ²⁴ If a kingdom is divided against itself, that kingdom cannot stand. ²⁵ If a house is divided against itself, that house cannot stand. ²⁶ And if Satan opposes himself and is divided, he cannot stand; his end has come. ²⁷ In fact, no one can enter a strong man's house without first tying him up. Then he can plunder the strong man's house. ²⁸ Truly I tell you, people can be forgiven all their sins and every slander they utter, ²⁹ but whoever blasphemes against the Holy Spirit will never be forgiven; they are guilty of an eternal sin." ³⁰ He said this because they were saying, "He has an impure spirit." (Mark 3:20-30, NIV®)

Parallel passages: Matthew 9:32-34; Luke 11:14-20

Mark 3:20-21: So many people were coming to Jesus that He and His disciples could not even eat a meal. News of His miraculous deeds had stirred the intrigue of people in both His own country and the surrounding countries. *"He is out of his mind"* - His own family thought that Jesus was crazy. Their intent was to take Him home and care for Him as best they could. It is unclear how they expected to bring Him home in the midst

of the great crowd of people - much less what they would do when the crowds would undoubtedly come to their house.

Mark 3:22: *"He is possessed by Beelzebub!"* – The religious leaders accused Jesus of being demon-possessed. And not just by any demon, but they thought Jesus was possessed by the devil himself (Beelzebub was a term used of Satan). Somehow they reasoned that it could only be the devil who was powerful enough to drive out demons. This is interesting in a couple of ways. One, it shows the gross lack of faith on their part. They did not consider that God could be strong enough to perform these miracles, only the devil. Secondly, it shows the hypocrisy of their position. Their own people in the religious leadership ranks sometimes cast out demons. So did they attribute their own work to the devil as well? Of course they did not. One of our own problems, not just these religious leaders in the 1st century, is that our standard for judgment is very low in our own eyes compared to how we judge others. Jesus clearly spoke against this:

> *[1]"Do not judge, or you too will be judged. [2] For in the same way you judge others, you will be judged, and with the measure you use, it will be measured to you. [3] "Why do you look at the speck of sawdust in your brother's eye and pay no attention to the plank in your own eye? [4] How can*

> *you say to your brother, 'Let me take the speck out of your eye,' when all the time there is a plank in your own eye? [5] You hypocrite, first take the plank out of your own eye, and then you will see clearly to remove the speck from your brother's eye. (Matthew 7:1-5, NIV®)*

Had the religious leaders applied the same standard, they would have lost credibility with the Jewish community and quite possibly their position. So they made the unequal judgment about Jesus and hoped no one would dare to question them. As far as we know from the biblical record, no one did criticize them.

Mark 3:23-30: Jesus pointed out the obvious to them: If the devil drives out his own demons, then he has no power. His kingdom cannot continue that way. This analogy can be applied to countries, organizations, communities, marriages, families, and even churches. Unity is critical. Where there is division, the entity will fail. At best it will fail to accomplish its mission.

He goes on with another analogy of a strong man's house that is robbed. It cannot happen unless you first bind up the strong man. Since the context is demon possession, the point is that neither the devil nor his demons could enter and possess a person unless that person was *"tied up"* first. A person would have to be very weak spiritually, far from God, for this to

 Insight Bible Commentary Series

happen. And God would have to permit this (as we see in the example of Job, the devil's authority is limited by God. Ref. Job 1:9-12, 2:2-6). In the life of a believer, it would not be possible for the devil to uproot the Holy Spirit who permanently indwells the believer from the moment of salvation (ref. John 14:17; Rom. 5:5, 8:9; Eph. 1:13-14). Nevertheless, a believer can be demonized, or attacked by demonic spirits - hence the need for spiritual armor (Eph. 6:10-18).

Mark 3:28-29: *"Eternal sin" (v. 29)* - This is also called the unpardonable sin. The unpardonable sin has been the subject of much debate as to the meaning. Some say that if you ever deny anything the Holy Spirit has done, then you have committed the unpardonable sin. But this would mean that anytime we sin, we would commit the unpardonable sin - for the Holy Spirit continually convicts people of sin, righteousness, and judgment (John 16:8-10). Others try to name certain heinous sins (e.g. murder, suicide, etc.) as the unpardonable sin. But the preceding verse in Mark 3:28 affirms that all sins and even blasphemies will be forgiven. There is only one consistent meaning for the unpardonable sin: persistent rebellion against the witness of the Holy Spirit concerning Jesus (John 15:26). Jesus was walking before the people of Israel performing miracles that only God could do. The religious leaders flatly refused to acknowledge that Jesus had come from God as the Messiah. In this passage, they denied that Jesus had driven out demons by the power of God (the Holy Spirit working in and through Jesus). Those who continued in this denial would indeed be guilty of the unpardonable sin.

Here is why. If you continue to deny that Jesus is the Messiah (Christ), then you too have committed the unpardonable sin. You have rejected God's provision of grace for all your sins. If one will not accept the grace of the LORD Jesus, as testified to every person by the Holy Spirit, then all that is left is God's righteous judgment. And without the grace of the LORD Jesus, no one will be found innocent in God's perfect judgment.

Through Jesus, God offers us eternal life. Without Him, we face eternal death - separation from His love and His presence in Hell. This is a stern warning for all who waver in belief about Jesus. The religious leaders of Jesus' time saw the miracles first hand and received this warning. How much more should you and I take note of this warning 2,000 years later?

(4) Jesus shares a close relationship with those who do God's will (Mark 3:31-35).

> *31 Then Jesus' mother and brothers arrived. Standing outside, they sent someone in to call*

him. ³² A crowd was sitting around him, and they told him, "Your mother and brothers are outside looking for you." ³³ "Who are my mother and my brothers?" he asked. ³⁴ Then he looked at those seated in a circle around him and said, "Here are my mother and my brothers! ³⁵ Whoever does God's will is my brother and sister and mother." (Mark 3:31-35, NIV®)

In what seems to be a rude response we find an important teaching by Jesus. There was a crowd in the house with Jesus and He was teaching them, as was His custom. His mother and brothers arrived to take charge of Him. So they sent someone to call Jesus out. Jesus responded by using this as a very teachable moment.

Parallel passages: Matthew 12:46-50; Luke 8:19-21

Mark 3:31-32: *"Jesus' mother and brothers" (v. 31)* – Mary was the virgin mother of Jesus. After Jesus was born, she had normal marital relations with Joseph and gave birth to other siblings. Technically, they were half-brothers of Jesus since Joseph was not the biological father of Jesus. Note that nothing is mentioned in the gospel record about Joseph after Jesus' childhood. Many presume that Joseph had passed away because he is never mentioned.

Mark 3:33-35: *"Who are my mother and my brothers?" (v. 33)* - This rhetorical question elicited curiosity among the crowd. His literal mother and brothers were outside calling Jesus to come to them. Jesus looked at those who had already come close to Him in the room and announced *"Here are my mother and my brothers!" (v. 34)* This was not intended as a rude remark but to make a point. Those who are close to Jesus, like a mother or a sibling, are *"Whoever does God's will." (v. 35)* His literal mother and brothers outside thought Jesus was crazy. But those inside were in a circle around Jesus, soaking in every word Jesus said. Jesus made it clear that it was not in the hearing or believing His words that people became close to Him. It is in the doing of God's word (ref. James 1:22-25). Those outside the house were not even hearing His words. Those inside heard and some believed. But only those who would then carry out Jesus' commands would enjoy close fellowship with the LORD Jesus.

 Insight Bible Commentary Series

IV. Jesus Prepares His Disciples (Mark 4:1-6:6)

A. Jesus teaches His disciples through parables (Mark 4:1-34).

Jesus spends time with the crowds teaching them various aspects of the kingdom of God. In these passages, He covers the parable of the sower of seed, parable of the growing seeds, and the parable of the mustard seed. All of these parables relate to how the kingdom of God grows.

(1) Parable of the sower (Mark 4:1-9).

> [1] *Again Jesus began to teach by the lake. The crowd that gathered around him was so large that he got into a boat and sat in it out on the lake, while all the people were along the shore at the water's edge.* [2] *He taught them many things by parables, and in his teaching said:* [3] *"Listen! A farmer went out to sow his seed.* [4] *As he was scattering the seed, some fell along the path, and the birds came and ate it up.* [5] *Some fell on rocky places, where it did not have much soil. It sprang up quickly, because the soil was shallow.* [6] *But when the sun came up, the plants were scorched, and they withered because they had no root.* [7] *Other seed fell among thorns, which grew up and choked the plants, so that they did not bear grain.* [8] *Still other seed fell on good soil. It came up,*

 Insight Bible Commentary Series

grew and produced a crop, some multiplying thirty, some sixty, some a hundred times." ⁹ *Then Jesus said, "Whoever has ears to hear, let them hear." (Mark 4:1-9, NIV®)*

As another crowd gathered around Jesus, He began teaching them *"by parables." (Mark 4:2, NIV®)* A parable is simply a story with one primary meaning. Those who have *"ears to hear" (Mark 4:9, NIV®)* are those who are seeking God and His truth. These will understand the spiritual truth being taught in the parable. Those who were listening merely to see Jesus perform a miracle would miss the main point of the parable. It would be an entertaining story with no spiritual significance to them.

Parallel passages: Matthew 13:1-9, Luke 8:4-8

Mark 4:1: Jesus used all means available to teach people, even to the point of having a floating pulpit.

Mark 4:2: *"He taught them many things by parables..." (NIV®)* It is extremely important to interpret a parable properly. There is one main point being conveyed by the parable. One spiritual truth can be gleaned from the teaching of a parable. Many take every single item referenced in a parable and try to interpret them in various ways. Jesus simply used examples from everyday life to illustrate the spiritual truth He wished to convey.

While there are different ways a truth can be applied, there is still only one central truth. As you go through different stages of life, you may find different ways to apply that truth - but there is still one basic truth in the parable.

Mark 4:3-7: In this parable, the seed is scattered along the ground and reaches different places. The first three places the seed reaches are not conducive to growth. The seed bears no fruit.

Mark 4:8: *"Still other seed fell on good soil" (NIV®)* – While the seed is scattered many places, only those places that have soil both prepared to receive and ready to make use of the seed will bear fruit. What was the difference in the seed sown by the sower in these various places? No difference - it was the same seed. What makes the difference in the crop produced by this seed? The condition of the soil makes the difference. Only in the case of *"good soil" (Mark 4:8, NIV®)* was there a crop that grew from the seed. So the parable is not about the sower sowing the seed, where he sows or how he sows. It is about the condition of the soil. The meaning of this parable is explained by Jesus in Mark 4:13-20.

Mark 4:9: *"ears to hear" (NIV®)* – Is it possible to listen without hearing? Of course it is. If we have no interest in what

is being said, we can hear it through the ears but not process the information in the brain. Hearing requires more than the sound going through the auditory faculties of the body. One must process and respond to what is heard. The difference the word of God makes in a person's life is not just the quality or the quantity of it but the condition of a person's heart in hearing the word.

(2) Jesus explains His use of parables (Mark 4:10-12).

> [10] *When he was alone, the Twelve and the others around him asked him about the parables.* [11] *He told them, "The secret of the kingdom of God has been given to you. But to those on the outside everything is said in parables* [12] *so that, "'they may be ever seeing but never perceiving, and ever hearing but never understanding; otherwise they might turn and be forgiven!'" (Mark 4:10-12, NIV®)*

Jesus explains His use of parables to teach people about the kingdom of God. Because the hearts of so many had become hard toward God, the truth of the kingdom was provided in parable form. The parables were simple enough for a child to understand. The truth was plain if you were open to hearing the truth from God.

Parallel passages: Matthew 13:10-17, Luke 8:9-10

Mark 4:10: Privately Jesus explained the meaning and application of the spiritual truths He taught through parables.

Mark 4:11: *"The secret of the kingdom of God" (NIV®)* – Jesus is the secret. He is the fulfillment of the Old Testament prophecies concerning Messiah and the intent of the Law itself (Matthew 5:17).

"But to those on the outside" – People had specific ideas about Messiah, His mission and character. Most people during this time saw Messiah as a political or military leader who would conquer Rome and establish Jerusalem as the capital of the world. Jesus certainly did not fit this mold at all. Those who wanted a Messiah to relieve their suffering and turn the tables on their enemies rejected Jesus because He did not conform to their idea of what Messiah should be and do. As a result, they remained outside the kingdom of God. The only way to enter the kingdom of God is through Jesus (John 14:6; Acts 4:12).

The parables illustrated truths about the kingdom of God. Without a willingness to accept the King of the kingdom of God, how can anyone understand His kingdom? The answer is that you cannot understand God's kingdom without accepting His King, the LORD Jesus. The people on the outside are those who refused to accept Jesus as Messiah (Christ). The disciples of

Insight Bible Commentary Series

Jesus, for the most part, were kingdom individuals. They had accepted Jesus as the Messiah (Christ) who *"who takes away the sin of the world!" (John 1:29, NIV®)* Since their hearts and their minds embraced Jesus as the Messiah, they were able to understand spiritual truths about the kingdom of God.

It is not a question about fairness but about Jesus trying to engage people in a way they could understand if they were willing to accept Him. If they were only interested in hearing a nice story or see an entertaining miracle, they would miss the whole point. For believers today we face the same issue. Do not let your neighbors, friends, and family miss the point. Connect the dots between Jesus, life, death, and eternity with your own life parables.

Mark 4:12: *"Otherwise they might turn and be forgiven!" (NIV®)* – Jesus reinforces this explanation by quoting the prophet Isaiah (Isaiah 6:9-10). It seems as though God is forsaking these hard-hearted people. But God has done His part in reaching out to the whole world through Jesus. Remember that God always desires a relationship with people - He loves everyone (John 3:16). He has made it clear that if you seek Him you will find Him. But the seeking must be from the heart - sincere and not for selfish purposes (ref. Jeremiah 29:13;

Proverbs 8:17; Acts 17:27). Those who continue to reject His grace will eventually become so dull toward spiritual truth that they simply will be unable to accept Jesus at all.

It seems rather cold to us that God would hide the truth from people. But that is not what is happening. The truth is being expressed very plainly, using examples from life that the hearers knew very well. In fact, because the spiritual truth was being taught so simply, most hard-hearted individuals would simply overlook it. Those whose hearts were hard would not bother to try and understand the spiritual truth in even the simplest parable. But those who sought to know the LORD would catch the central meaning.

(3) Jesus explains the parable of the Sower (Mark 4:13-20).

> *[13] Then Jesus said to them, "Don't you understand this parable? How then will you understand any parable? [14] The farmer sows the word. [15] Some people are like seed along the path, where the word is sown. As soon as they hear it, Satan comes and takes away the word that was sown in them. [16] Others, like seed sown on rocky places, hear the word and at once receive it with joy. [17] But since they have no root, they last only a short time. When trouble or persecution comes because of the word, they quickly fall away. [18] Still others, like seed sown among thorns, hear the word; [19] but the worries of this life, the deceitfulness of*

wealth and the desires for other things come in and choke the word, making it unfruitful. ^{20} Others, like seed sown on good soil, hear the word, accept it, and produce a crop—some thirty, some sixty, some a hundred times what was sown." (Mark 4:13-20, NIV®)

Jesus explains the parable of the sower to His disciples. First He admonishes them for failing to understand the parable. Apparently the disciples were not searching hard enough to understand the spiritual significance of what Jesus told them. So Jesus had to give them the meaning in small portions.

Parallel passages: Matthew 13:18-23, Luke 8:11-15

Mark 4:14: *"The farmer sows the word" (NIV®)* – This is a symbol of people spreading the word of God as they go through life. Sometimes it is spread through formal settings, such as a church service or radio program. Most often it is one believer talking to a neighbor, teammate, or anyone else they encounter in the course of their life. The truth of God's word is shared. However, this is not the focus of the parable. The main point is the receptivity of the hearer.

Mark 4:15: *"Seed along the path" (NIV®)* – Seed sown along the path cannot grow at all. There is no soil for the seed there. This represents people with hard hearts who are centered on themselves alone. They hear the word but it bounces off because of their hardness toward God. Figuratively speaking, they give the word of God no chance to grow.

"Satan comes" (NIV®) – The devil tempts the person with other things to draw their attention away from the word. Thus he *"takes away the word that was sown in them." (NIV®)* They forget what they heard and move on.

Mark 4:16-17: *"Seed sown on rocky places" (Mark 4:16, NIV®)* – There is soil in the rocky places for seed to begin growing. But there is not enough for the plant to be viable. A solid root cannot be formed. The people represented here are emotional or entertainment-driven individuals. They ride whatever wave comes along. Their attention span to any one thing is very short. These are individuals that may get caught up in the fellowship and worship of a church or group of Christians. But they are moving on feelings not faith. Their commitment is to the entertainment and when the road gets rough, they move on to something else. You may have seen individuals like this who make professions of faith in Christ over and over and over. These people have an emotional experience to the word but do not really accept it as God's eternal truth - truth to be believed and obeyed no matter what. It sounds good to them and they are

 Insight Bible Commentary Series

happy with it. But when it becomes inconvenient or causes them trouble, they reject it.

"They quickly fall away" (Mark 4:17, NIV®) – This is not a reference to losing salvation. The people in this category had no root and, thus, never bore any fruit. You cannot lose what you do not already possess. These people never believed the word. They heard it and had an emotional experience. But the word never took root in their heart and mind.

Mark 4:18-19: *"Seed sown among thorns" (Mark 4:18, NIV®)* – Seed that is sown among the thorns (or weeds) starts to grow but quickly gets choked out. The nutrients and water in the soil are stolen away by the thorns, as is the light from the sun. The plant never thrives to the point of bearing fruit. People in this category also hear the word but give it little priority in their lives. They are consumed with other things - gaining wealth, acquiring material things, pursuing pleasure, or worrying about what may happen next. These people may also have professed faith in the LORD Jesus. Because their priority is on material issues in life rather than eternal issues, they never believe or obey the word. As a result, their attention to worldly things has the effect to *"choke the word, making it unfruitful." (Mark 4:19, NIV®)* They bear no fruit from believing and obeying God. Jesus indicated that those who believe in Him and follow Him will bear fruit (John 15:5) with eternal consequences (John 15:8). He also indicated that those who profess to know Him and His word but bear no fruit (or bad fruit) demonstrate that they have no connection to Him at all (ref. Matthew 7:16-20). *"Thus, by their fruit you will recognize them." (Matthew 7:20, NIV®)* The people in this category are not believers either.

Mark 4:20: *"Seed sown on good soil" (NIV®)* – Seed sown in good soil takes root, grows, endures storms, and eventually bears fruit. One seed multiplies to bear much fruit. So it is with the person who hears the word, believes it, and obeys it. The spiritual truth takes root and creates good fruit in the life of the believers. The fruit will be the *"fruit of the Spirit is love, joy, peace, patience, kindness, goodness, faithfulness, gentleness and self-control." (Galatians 5:22-23, NIV®)* The fruit will also be the good works that God has planned for every person who believes in Him (Ephesians 2:10).

Note that the same seed is sown in all cases. It is not a deficiency in the word at all. The issue is how receptive a person is to hearing the word. In only one case was fruit born out of the seed that was sown. If one were to apply this parable to spreading the gospel of Jesus Christ, then only the last group of people, *"seed sown on good soil" (NIV®)*, represent people who

become Christians – born again into the family of God (John 3:3). But the word in this parable represents more than just the gospel – it is all spiritual truth from God that is shared in life. God's word will bear fruit in the life of anyone who hears it, believes it, and obeys God.

(4) Jesus announces the keys to understanding the Kingdom of God (Mark 4:21-25).

> *21 He said to them, "Do you bring in a lamp to put it under a bowl or a bed? Instead, don't you put it on its stand? 22 For whatever is hidden is meant to be disclosed, and whatever is concealed is meant to be brought out into the open. 23 If anyone has ears to hear, let them hear." 24 "Consider carefully what you hear," he continued. "With the measure you use, it will be measured to you—and even more. 25 Whoever has will be given more; whoever does not have, even what they have will be taken from them." (Mark 4:21-25, NIV®)*

Parallel passages: Luke 8:16-18 (similarities to Matthew 5:15, 10:26, 7:2, 13:12)

Mark 4:21-25: The kingdom of God presented by Jesus is not intended to be a secret to the world. Rather, it is to be brought into the light for all to see. Jesus is the secret to the kingdom of God and to understanding it. The disciples accepted Jesus as the Messiah and, as a result, had the key to understanding the parables. They were *"good soil"* for the seeds of God's word – all except for Judas Iscariot.

There are two related keys to understanding the kingdom:

i. Truth must be proclaimed - Using the example of a lamp, Jesus shows that no one lights a lamp and then covers it up. Similarly, the truth He taught must be proclaimed to the world. Those who had the *"ear to hear"* – seeking to know God – will hear and understand. God has promised that *"You will seek me and find me when you seek me with all your heart." (Jeremiah 29:13, NIV®)*

ii. Truth must be received – There is a two-fold responsibility regarding the truth. It must also be received by the listener. Listening with an obedient heart is the key. *"Consider carefully what you hear" (v. 24)* – One must be prudent in what you hear for many false teachers are ready to pollute your understanding of God. The more truth from God's word you absorb, the greater your understanding. God will bless your sincere efforts to learn with *"even more." (v. 24)* Conversely, those who reject (or refuse to obey)

what they hear will lose their understanding. This is an important warning to every believer to keep growing in both the grace and the knowledge of our Lord Jesus (2 Peter 3:18).

Mark 4:24: The key to understanding God and His kingdom is in listening to God's word. If you really hear and respond to what you hear, you will grow in grace and knowledge of Him.

Mark 4:25: In God's kingdom, if you listen, your faith will grow. If you do not listen, your faith will diminish.

(5) Parable of the growing seed (Mark 4:26-29).

> *^{26} He also said, "This is what the kingdom of God is like. A man scatters seed on the ground. ^{27} Night and day, whether he sleeps or gets up, the seed sprouts and grows, though he does not know how. ^{28} All by itself the soil produces grain—first the stalk, then the head, then the full kernel in the head. ^{29} As soon as the grain is ripe, he puts the sickle to it, because the harvest has come." (Mark 4:26-29, NIV®)*

Mark 4:26-29: Jesus shares a parable to illustrate the growth of the kingdom of God in individuals. Once the sower has planted the seed, it grows. The sower does not know how. When we share the word of God with people, it takes root in some and grows. We do not know how it works but God causes the truth to sink in and have its effect. When the seed of the word grows in a person, that person eventually bears fruit. Our duty is to sow the word and watch God's marvelous and mysterious work in bringing growth to those who hear.

(6) Parable of the mustard seed (Mark 4:30-32).

> *³⁰ Again he said, "What shall we say the kingdom of God is like, or what parable shall we use to describe it? ³¹ It is like a mustard seed, which is the smallest of all seeds on earth. ³² Yet when planted, it grows and becomes the largest of all garden plants, with such big branches that the birds can perch in its shade." (Mark 4:30-32, NIV®)*

Parallel passages: Matthew 13:31-32, Luke 13:18-19

Mark 4:30-32: In another parable, Jesus shows a different aspect of the kingdom of God - God's rule in the world He made and in the lives of His people. A *"mustard seed" (v. 31)* was the smallest seed known in that region of the world. But when planted in fertile soil it became a very tall shrub. It was so large that even the birds could *"perch in its shade." (v. 32)*

Many commentators have drawn various conclusions from different aspects of this parable. But keep in mind that parables have one main point. Clearly the main point here is the

extent of growth from something very small. God's rule in the world starts small in people with His general revelation from nature. The creation tells us there must be a Creator (Psalm 19:1-4; Romans 1:18-20). As the word of God is then revealed to a person, God's rule forms in an incredibly significant way. Faith starts small but permeates the whole of a person. The same is true for the world. One day God's rule will encompass the entire world even though it started with Jesus and just a few of His disciples. This is the main point of the mustard seed parable. Anything beyond that is speculation and potentially adds to what Jesus plainly said. It is more important to grasp the main truth and put it into practice than to grasp for subtle meanings with no solid biblical support.

(7) Jesus uses parables for the people but explains all to His disciples (Mark 4:33-34).

> [33] *With many similar parables Jesus spoke the word to them, as much as they could understand.* [34] *He did not say anything to them without using a parable. But when he was alone with his own disciples, he explained everything. (Mark 4:33-34, NIV®)*

Parallel passages: Matthew 13:34

Mark 4:33-34: Jesus continues to teach the people who gathered around Him, *"as much as they could understand." (v. 33)* There is a limit to how much one can learn at one time. Understanding God's truth is no different. Rather than try to absorb much information in a short time, it is better to study and apply small amounts on a regular basis. Learn God's truth and obey what you learn – then move on to the next topic.

"He did not say anything to them without using a parable." (v. 34) The parables were not meant to make the learning process difficult. On the contrary, the parables engaged the mind and hearts of the listeners. The stories used common things and events from the 1st century, but typically with a twist. The hearers would be drawn into the story and, while there, they would find an important spiritual truth. Those who sought to know the LORD would get that truth. God would reveal it to them. Those that had no interest in God would only hear a curious but entertaining story. Fortunately for His disciples, Jesus *"explained everything" (v. 34)* privately.

B. Jesus teaches His disciples through miracles (Mark 4:35-6:6).

(1) Jesus calms the wind and the sea (Mark 4:35-41).

> *^{35} That day when evening came, he said to his disciples, "Let us go over to the other side." ^{36} Leaving the crowd behind, they took him along, just as he was, in the boat. There were also other boats with him. ^{37} A furious squall came up, and the waves broke over the boat, so that it was nearly swamped. ^{38} Jesus was in the stern, sleeping on a cushion. The disciples woke him and said to him, "Teacher, don't you care if we drown?" ^{39} He got up, rebuked the wind and said to the waves, "Quiet! Be still!" Then the wind died down and it was completely calm. ^{40} He said to his disciples, "Why are you so afraid? Do you still have no faith?" ^{41} They were terrified and asked each other, "Who is this? Even the wind and the waves obey him!" (Mark 4:35-41, NIV®)*

Parallel passages: Matthew 8:23-27, Luke 8:22-25

Mark 4:35-41: After a fruitful day of teaching, Jesus led His disciples to cross over the Sea of Galilee. His goal was to reach as many people as He could with the good news of the kingdom (Mark 1:38). They crossed the sea in several boats. Jesus was weary from preaching and teaching all day so He slept.

"A furious squall came up" (v. 37) – The Sea of Galilee is known for storms developing rapidly on the open waters. It can appear calm one moment and then turn into a raging storm the next. It is a very dangerous condition and the disciples' boat nearly turned over. They woke up their Master asking, *"Teacher, don't you care if we drown?" (v. 38)* Instead of letting Jesus know the storm was endangering everyone, they selfishly accused Him of failing to care for their own lives. Their question indicates a lack of concern for Jesus Himself. Of course, as fishermen they knew all too well the dangers of this storm.

Out of a dead sleep, Jesus woke up and ordered the wind and the waves to become calm again. As the Creator of all things (John 1:3; Hebrews 1:2; Colossians 1:16), Jesus is able to change any condition of creation He chooses. It was an incredible miracle from a human perspective – but an easy thing for the Creator. The point was to show the disciples more than simply His care for their well-being. He wanted them to realize His divine nature and power. If you are with the Creator, nothing in all creation should ever scare you. And so Jesus asked them, *"Why are you so afraid? Do you still have no faith?" (v. 40)* The disciples were with Jesus and knew He was someone very special. They knew God was with Him. They did not yet

 Insight Bible Commentary Series

understand that as both God and man, Jesus was *"Immanuel ... 'God with us.'" (Matthew 1:23, NIV®)* Lacking faith, they were terrified at the power Jesus commanded (v. 41).

(2) Jesus drives out a legion of demons into a herd of pigs (Mark 5:1-20).

> *[1] They went across the lake to the region of the Gerasenes. [2] When Jesus got out of the boat, a man with an impure spirit came from the tombs to meet him. [3] This man lived in the tombs, and no one could bind him anymore, not even with a chain. [4] For he had often been chained hand and foot, but he tore the chains apart and broke the irons on his feet. No one was strong enough to subdue him. [5] Night and day among the tombs and in the hills he would cry out and cut himself with stones. [6] When he saw Jesus from a distance, he ran and fell on his knees in front of him. [7] He shouted at the top of his voice, "What do you want with me, Jesus, Son of the Most High God? In God's name don't torture me!" [8] For Jesus had said to him, "Come out of this man, you impure spirit!" [9] Then Jesus asked him, "What is your name?" "My name is Legion," he replied, "for we are many." [10] And he begged Jesus again and again not to send them out of the area. [11] A large herd of pigs was feeding on the nearby hillside. [12] The demons begged Jesus, "Send us among the pigs; allow us to go into them." [13] He gave them permission, and the impure spirits came out and went into the pigs. The herd, about two thousand in number, rushed down the steep bank into the*

lake and were drowned. ¹⁴ *Those tending the pigs ran off and reported this in the town and countryside, and the people went out to see what had happened.* ¹⁵ *When they came to Jesus, they saw the man who had been possessed by the legion of demons, sitting there, dressed and in his right mind; and they were afraid.* ¹⁶ *Those who had seen it told the people what had happened to the demon-possessed man—and told about the pigs as well.* ¹⁷ *Then the people began to plead with Jesus to leave their region.* ¹⁸ *As Jesus was getting into the boat, the man who had been demon-possessed begged to go with him.* ¹⁹ *Jesus did not let him, but said, "Go home to your own people and tell them how much the Lord has done for you, and how he has had mercy on you."* ²⁰ *So the man went away and began to tell in the Decapolis how much Jesus had done for him. And all the people were amazed. (Mark 5:1-20, NIV®)*

Parallel passages: Matthew 8:28-34, Luke 8:26-39

Mark 5:1: *"Region of the Gerasenes" (NIV®)* - Different manuscripts have slight variations of Gerasenes: Gadarenes, and Gergesenes. They all refer to an area in the southeast corner of the Sea of Galilee. It was an area heavily populated with non-Jewish people as evidenced by the flocks of pigs that were kept (Mark 5:11). Pigs were considered unclean under the Law of Moses (Leviticus 11:7-8).

Mark 5:2-5: A man met Jesus as He got out of the boat. The man had *"an evil spirit." (v2)* This was also called an unclean

 Insight Bible Commentary Series

spirit. He was demonized - under the influence of fallen angels. The fallen angels (or demons) are the ones that followed Lucifer in rebellion against God. Sometimes this is called demon-possession but the use of the phrase is inconsistent. Possession implies ownership and the demons own no human beings. God, as the Creator of all, owns all.

Yet people can allow themselves to be influenced by demonic spirits in sometimes spectacular ways. The demon-possessed man demonstrated great strength by breaking the chains apart on his hands and feet (v. 4). The demons tortured the man. He would *"cut himself with stones," (v. 5)* causing him to live in the tombs of dead people (v. 3). The demonic influence over this man was powerful.

Mark 5:6-10: As the demonized man approached, Jesus recognized an evil spirit within him. He commanded the evil spirit to leave (v. 8). The demon resisted – begging Jesus not to torture him. Note that the demon acknowledged what the disciples had yet to learn: Jesus is the *"Son of the Most High God." (v. 7)*

In an unusual personal touch, Jesus asked the demon his name. It is difficult to accept, perhaps, but these demons are fallen angels who were created by God. He loves them even though they rebelled against Him. The demon replied, *"Legion ... for we are many." (v. 9)* Jesus was speaking with the lead demon who spoke for the group.

Note in verse 10: *"He begged Jesus again and again not to send them out of the area."* Some have proposed that demons are territorial. They surmise from this verse that demons tend to stay in a certain geographic area. This verse certainly lends credence to that view. Keep in mind that demons and angels are spirit beings – not confined to physical space as humans are.

Mark 5:11-13: The demons requested that they be allowed to leave the man but enter the herd of pigs nearby. This shows that demons can influence animals as well as people. As the entered the large herd of pigs, they caused them to run down the hill and into a lake where they drowned. This did not kill the demons since they are spirit beings. Presumably they stayed in that area to torment other people.

Mark 5:14-17: The witnesses to this event (those tending the pigs) ran to the town to tell them. This brought many people from the town to see if it was true. Their previous reaction to the demon possessed man was fear, understandably. But now that he was free of the demons and in his right mind, they were still afraid. Once the witnesses explained what had happened, they

were afraid of Jesus as well. Consider the enormous influence of the demons on the people of this area – they were living in fear. They begged even Jesus to leave them. Perhaps they were afraid of losing more pigs. It seems more likely that the depth of spiritual darkness the demons in this area had managed to convey. The people were not thinking clearly either – they were more afraid of the work of the demons that the One who had command over the demons. They could not have thought Jesus to be demonized and they saw the formerly demon-possessed man in his right mind. So they had a bright spiritual light shining in their community but preferred darkness instead (ref. John 3:19).

Mark 5:18-20: The man who had been set free by Jesus wanted to go with Him. Jesus, however, wanted him to remain and evangelize this area he had previously tormented. The formerly demon-possessed man had a huge task to share the good news in a spiritually depressed area. But he also had an amazing story to share – a life completely changed by an encounter with Jesus. Through his life change and his message, he would capture the attention of many people. Many people were undoubtedly saved as a result of his witness. He simply had to follow Jesus' command, *"tell them how much the Lord has done for you, and how he has had mercy on you." (v. 19)*

"Decapolis" (v. 20) – This means the "ten cities." The Decapolis was an area all around the southeast corner of the Sea of Galilee.

(3) Jesus heals the sick and raises the dead (Mark 5:21-43).

[21] When Jesus had again crossed over by boat to the other side of the lake, a large crowd gathered around him while he was by the lake. [22] Then one of the synagogue leaders, named Jairus, came, and when he saw Jesus, he fell at his feet. [23] He pleaded earnestly with him, "My little daughter is dying. Please come and put your hands on her so that she will be healed and live." [24] So Jesus went with him. A large crowd followed and pressed around him. [25] And a woman was there who had been subject to bleeding for twelve years. [26] She had suffered a great deal under the care of many doctors and had spent all she had, yet instead of getting better she grew worse. [27] When she heard about Jesus, she came up behind him in the crowd and touched his cloak, [28] because she thought, "If I just touch his clothes, I will be healed." [29] Immediately her bleeding stopped and she felt in her body that she was freed from her suffering. [30] At once Jesus realized that power had gone out from him. He turned around in the crowd and asked, "Who touched my clothes?" [31] "You see the people crowding against you," his disciples answered, "and yet you can ask, 'Who touched me?'" [32] But Jesus kept looking around to see who had done it. [33] Then the woman, knowing what had happened to her, came and fell at his feet and, trembling with fear, told him the whole

truth. *34* He said to her, "Daughter, your faith has healed you. Go in peace and be freed from your suffering." *35* While Jesus was still speaking, some people came from the house of Jairus, the synagogue leader. "Your daughter is dead," they said. "Why bother the teacher anymore?" *36* Overhearing what they said, Jesus told him, "Don't be afraid; just believe." *37* He did not let anyone follow him except Peter, James and John the brother of James. *38* When they came to the home of the synagogue leader, Jesus saw a commotion, with people crying and wailing loudly. *39* He went in and said to them, "Why all this commotion and wailing? The child is not dead but asleep." *40* But they laughed at him. After he put them all out, he took the child's father and mother and the disciples who were with him, and went in where the child was. *41* He took her by the hand and said to her, "Talitha koum!" (which means "Little girl, I say to you, get up!"). *42* Immediately the girl stood up and began to walk around (she was twelve years old). At this they were completely astonished. *43* He gave strict orders not to let anyone know about this, and told them to give her something to eat. (Mark 5:21-43, NIV®)*

Parallel passages: Matthew 9:18-26, Luke 8:40-56

Jesus left the region of the Gerasenes and cross back over the Sea of Galilee. He was approached by one of the synagogue leaders, Jairus, because his daughter was dying. He pleaded with

Jesus to come to his house to heal her. On the way a woman was healed by touching Jesus' cloak. At Jairus' house, Jesus found the girl had already died. But Jesus took three of His closest disciples with Him into her room and raised her from the dead. Jesus demonstrated His power to heal the sick and even raise the dead to life.

Mark 5:21: *"Crossed over by boat"* – From the southeast side of the Sea of Galilee Jesus and His disciples crossed over to the west side. Once again, a large crowd of people arrived to see Jesus.

Mark 5:22-24a: As a synagogue ruler, Jairus would have taken a chance of being criticized or, perhaps, even removed from his position for going to Jesus. The religious community was opposed to the ministry of Jesus for a number of reasons:

- His teaching was not based on rabbinical tradition but on what the Scriptures actually said and meant. This created a level of resentment with the religious leaders.

- His popularity with the people threatened the authority of the religious leaders.

- His miracles were, for the most part, performed in public put the religious leaders in a terrible paradox. They did not want to lose their prominent and lucrative positions so they could not affirm Jesus as a

prophet of God. Yet His miracles could not be denied.

Jairus took the chance and went to Jesus anyway. When your child's life is in danger, it changes your priorities as a parent. The respect of the other religious leaders becomes much less important than saving your child's life. Jairus was willing to risk it all. He *"fell at His feet,"* (v. 22) prostrating himself before Jesus. Apparently, Jairus had witnessed Jesus healing the sick. And Jairus knew his daughter was dying for he asked, *"so that she will be healed and live."* (v. 23) Jairus *"pleaded earnestly"* (v. 23) and Jesus went with Jairus to His house.

Mark 5:24b-26: As Jesus was traveling to Jairus' house, a woman pressed through the crowd to get to Him. She *"had been subject to bleeding"* (v. 25) for many years. The doctors of the 1st century were unable to help her. We can only speculate what the bleeding problem was – most commentators assume it was a disorder of the female organs. Whatever the cause, the woman had to have been weak from the loss of blood. Under Mosaic Law, she would have been considered "unclean" because of the bleeding – unable to worship at the Temple and ostracized from the orthodox Jewish community. It was both a health and a social problem for her.

Mark 5:27-29: The woman had faith in Jesus. She had heard and possibly seen His miracles of healing. So she approached Him secretly to touch His cloak. Most likely this was because she was aware of the ritual law violation of physically touching Jesus because of "uncleanness." The act would also make Jesus ritually unclean for seven days. So she *"came up behind Him in the crowd" (v. 27)* to touch His outer garment. She believed in Jesus' power to heal so much that she thought only one touch of His clothes would heal her. And it happened exactly that way. *"Immediately her bleeding stopped" (v. 29)* – the woman knew instantly that she was finally healed.

Mark 5:30: *"At once Jesus realized that power had gone out from Him" (v. 30)* – The woman was not the only one who knew she was healed. It was Jesus' power (the Greek word is "dunamis" from which we derive the English word "dynamite"). Innate power from within Jesus brought this woman healing. *"Who touched My clothes?" (v. 30)* – as God the Son, Jesus knew who had touched Him and who had received the healing. He wished to publicly confront the woman. The miracle had occurred already. Jesus wanted to strengthen the woman spiritually who was already healed physically.

Mark 5:31: The disciples must have been aggravated at Jesus' questions that seemed ridiculous to them. This is a good

 Insight Bible Commentary Series

example. In a large crowd walking with and behind Jesus, people touched Him constantly. Yet Jesus had a special purpose for this question, as He always did.

Mark 5:32-34: Jesus continued to look around, waiting for the woman to identify herself. It was not for Jesus that she needed to do this - it was for her own spiritual healing. Her body was healed but she needed to grow in faith. Jesus does not want "secret Christians" to follow Him. So He waited patiently for the woman to gather the courage to share the remarkably good news.

"... trembling with fear, told Him" (v. 33) - The woman was afraid to let everyone know that she, an unclean woman, had touched a holy man (Jesus). She may also have been afraid that she took the healing from Him without asking, as if such a thing were possible. But she shared the *"whole truth" (v. 33)* – telling of her years of suffering and the immediate healing touch of the LORD Jesus.

"Your faith has healed you" (v. 34) – Many have taken this verse out of context to mean that if you simply believe that you can be healed of any sickness without drugs or therapy. Some have gone so far as to deny themselves or their children necessary medical treatments so they can claim their healing by faith. And some have died as a result. Physical healing is not a guarantee in

this life but in Heaven. Some use *"by his wounds we are healed" (Isaiah 53:5, NIV®)* to argue that, through the cross of Christ, physical healing is a certainty. But the context of a sentence must drive the determination of the meaning - this applies to anything you hear or read. In the Isaiah 53 passage, it was for *"transgressions"* and *"iniquities"* that Jesus was wounded on the cross. So the healing is a spiritual healing. In the case of the woman with a bleeding problem, she had already been healed physically: *"Immediately her bleeding stopped." (v. 29)* So Jesus' statement *"your faith has healed you" (v. 34)* refers to her spiritual healing. Her faith had now gone public. She declared publicly her faith in Jesus and His power to heal. She had overcome her fear by faith and could now *"go in peace and be freed from your suffering." (v. 34)*

Mark 5:35-37: People from the community (where Jairus served as the synagogue leader) came to Jesus with the bad news: *"Your daughter is dead." (v. 35)* When Jairus had left to find Jesus, she was still alive. Now that she was dead, there was no hope from an earthly perspective. This was the attitude of the people: *"Why bother the Teacher [Jesus] anymore?" (v. 35)* Jesus had healed many sick people and even driven out demons. But once a person was dead, they reasoned that nothing else could be done.

 Insight Bible Commentary Series

No one had any hope that Jesus could raise the dead. Only God could accomplish such a miracle.

So Jesus comforted Jairus by saying *"Don't be afraid; just believe." (v. 36)* Jesus knew He was going to raise Jairus' daughter from the dead. But He did not tell Jairus. He simply asked Jairus to trust Him and believe in Him. That is what God always wants us to do. He does not lay out the specific future for us. He does not guarantee positive outcomes in every life event. But He does promise to be with us through it all (Matthew 28:20; Hebrews 13:5). God knows what is best in every situation. So we have to learn to trust in Him.

"Except Peter, James, and John" (v. 37) - These three disciples were in the inner circle of Jesus' discipleship efforts. Jesus had chosen twelve apostles already. But these three men were chosen for special mentoring and teaching. Jesus saw potential in these men that He did not see in the others. The extra time He spent with them helped to hone their understanding, leadership abilities, and their common vision for the kingdom of God. Sharing only with these three the amazing miracle He had planned was a great honor and learning experience. We would do well to learn the art of mentoring young people - sharing with

them our life experience (both the good and the bad) in following the LORD Jesus.

Mark 5:38-40a: *"Jesus saw a commotion" (v. 38)* – From the Greek word "thorubos" meaning a great clamor or disturbance driven by fear. The young girl had died. Death frightens everyone who has no assurance of what lies beyond the grave. Apart from a relationship with our Creator God, one cannot have this assurance. Because Jairus was the synagogue ruler, he had many friends and family members at the house. Many were crying and crying out loudly. Jesus' response to this hopeless situation gave some context to the girl's death: *"The child is not dead but asleep." (v. 39)* To the world she was dead. To her Creator, though, she was very much alive in spirit.

"But they laughed at Him" (v. 40) – Laughter seems an odd response to Jesus' hopeful comment. The Greek work "katagelao" translated "laughter" means a scornful laugh. They were mocking Jesus' response. Not knowing He is the Creator of all things (John 1:3; Colossians 1:16; Hebrews 1:2), their scorn is understandable.

Mark 5:40b-43: Jesus sent the mourners out of the house. For what He was about to do, Jesus wanted the complete attention of His disciples and the parents. Taking the dead girl by her hand,

 Insight Bible Commentary Series

Jesus said in Aramaic, *"Talitha koum!" (which means, "Little girl, I say to you, get up!") (v. 41)* Galileans of this time spoke both Aramaic and Greek. At times, Jesus would use Aramaic phrases in His ministry.

At the command of her Creator, the young girl rose from the dead. Standing and walking were evidence that she lived again. Jesus had only to speak the words and His power raised her. This is not what is spoken of later as the resurrection. In the future, when Jesus returns, the dead in Christ will be resurrected into an immortal body that will never grow old or die. But this young girl was raised to life in a mortal body since Jesus told them she needed *"something to eat." (v. 43)* She would grow up, grow old, and one day die again.

"He gave strict orders not to let anyone know about this" (v. 43) – Again, Jesus gives this very strange command (ref. Mark 1:43-45). Had the parents rushed to proclaim to everyone Jesus' miraculous raising of their daughter to life, Jesus would have been crushed by the crowds wanting a similar miracle for all of their loved ones who had died. Jesus' work was to proclaim the good news of the kingdom (Mark 1:14-15). The miracles confirmed the authenticity of His words and His identity as the Messiah (Christ).

Imagine the torment this command caused the parents. A million questions would come to them from everyone in the town. The girl was dead but now alive! It seemed almost cruel for Jesus to bind them with the command of secrecy. But all of God's commands are for our provision and protection. While any given command may seem temporarily burdensome, trust that God is accomplishing something greater in us and in His world. In this case, Peter, James, and John had learned a lesson about Jesus' power and identity they would never forget. While we do not know any more about Jairus, it is not hard to imagine the synagogue ruler and his wife became followers of Jesus as Messiah that very day.

We do see in Matthew 9:26 that word of this miracle spread through the community anyway. The crowd saw the dead girl in the house, saw Jesus go in, and saw the girl come out of the house alive whether her parents said anything or not. They figure out what happened and it was discussed throughout the community.

(4) Jesus heals only a few sick people in His hometown (Mark 6:1-6a).

> *¹ Jesus left there and went to his hometown, accompanied by his disciples. ² When the Sabbath came, he began to teach in the synagogue, and*

many who heard him were amazed. "Where did this man get these things?" they asked. "What's this wisdom that has been given him? What are these remarkable miracles he is performing? ³ Isn't this the carpenter? Isn't this Mary's son and the brother of James, Joseph, Judas and Simon? Aren't his sisters here with us?" And they took offense at him. ⁴ Jesus said to them, "A prophet is not without honor except in his own town, among his relatives and in his own home." ⁵ He could not do any miracles there, except lay his hands on a few sick people and heal them. ⁶ He was amazed at their lack of faith. (Mark 6:1-6a, NIV®)

Parallel passages: Matthew 13:53-58, related passage John 4:44

Mark 6:1-2a: Jesus and His disciples traveled to Nazareth where Jesus grew up. In Nazareth, the people had heard of the miracles performed by Jesus elsewhere. Now they expected to see them firsthand. *"When the Sabbath came, he began to teach" (v. 2)* – this was the custom of Jesus. He taught people whenever they gathered around Him but He also went to the gathering at the synagogue every Sabbath (Friday at sundown to Saturday at sundown by our modern calendar). His teaching *"amazed" (v. 2)* those who heard Him. It was amazing in several ways. First, it was the clearest teaching of God's word ever heard since it was given by God in the flesh, Jesus. It was also amazing because He taught it with authority. Unlike the other Rabbis (teachers of the Law), Jesus did not couch His words in the opinions of other scholarly Rabbis. He explained the meaning of God's word because He inspired its very writing through the prophets (ref. 1 Peter 1:10-11). Lastly, Jesus' teaching amazed the people because they knew Jesus from childhood. He had not spent years in training under the direction and mentoring of the rabbinical schools. He had not studied at a Bible college or seminary. Today, Jesus would not have been able to get a job as a pastor due to His lack of credentials. Nevertheless, His teaching was powerful and clear - utterly amazing to all who heard.

This is an important lesson for people today. God gives wisdom concerning His word through the Holy Spirit. Though Bible College and Seminary work are important steps in preparation for ministry, they are no substitute for the teaching of Jesus through personal study of God's word. Much of God's word is clear to those who take the time to read, reflect, and apply its teachings in daily life. Books can be helpful but are never to be a substitute for letting God speak to you directly through the study of the Bible.

Mark 6:2b-3: The amazement of the people quickly turned into bitter envy. They asked, *"Where did this man get these things?"* and *"What's this wisdom that has been given him..." (v. 2)* Since they knew He did not go through any formal training, they reasoned that someone must have handed Him some sermon notes. Or perhaps He copied the teaching of others. Apparently, they could not believe that anyone could learn God's word on His own – this was probably a cultural belief reinforced by the synagogue leaders. But they took offense as they realized this was the local carpenter expounding God's word to them. Their own conviction from God's word taught by the hometown boy turned into envy and jealousy. As a result, they refused to really listen to God's word and it had no impact on their lives. This is why some people can sit in church for years under solid Bible teaching without ever coming to know Jesus personally or growing in their faith. One must be open to learning and willing to apply what is learned. The distractions of life and the pride of life can easily block a person's understanding of Bible truths.

Mark 6:4: *"A prophet without honor" (v.4)* – Jesus had honored people but was not honored by them in His hometown. He was a prophet who was not honored by the people that knew Him from childhood. It is rare for a local person to assume the role of teacher/pastor over people that know him well. Locals know all your past sins and current faults. This casts a shadow over one's call to preach - and why God often calls people to minister in different places from their hometown.

Mark 6:5-6: *"He could not do any miracles there"* *(v. 5)* – This verse has led to some faulty interpretations regarding the nature of faith. Clearly it does not mean that Jesus could not do any miracles because He was unable to do so. Verse five says that He did heal several people. Some suggest that the people did not have enough faith to get the miracles. This has led to a dangerous error in the church called the "health and wealth" gospel. It goes like this:

> *God wants you to be healthy and wealthy. If you have enough faith, you can claim your healing or prosperity in Jesus' name and it will be done. Just speak the words of faith and you can create your own reality.*

Various verses are used as alleged proof texts including this passage in Mark. But a careful reading with rational thinking shows clearly this "health and wealth" teaching is in error. Jesus did heal people in spite of their lack of faith. Consider the account of the ten lepers, only one of which came back to express thanks and faith in the LORD Jesus (Luke 17:11-18). Ten were healed of a fatal disease but only one expressed faith in the LORD Jesus. Consider also that the one that was already healed came back to Jesus. It was this point that Jesus said, *"your faith has made you well."* (Luke 17:18, NIV®) So the final "healing" was a spiritual one not a physical one. Other

 Insight Bible Commentary Series

examples include a man at the Bethesda pools (John 5:1-15) and a mother's dead son (obviously without faith) who was raised to life (Luke 7:11-17). When the text says that Jesus *"could not do any miracles there" (v. 6)* it means in the sense that it would have made no difference. The miracles were a confirmation of His teaching. Since the people took offense at His very words. There was no point in doing miracles to confirm them. The people had already closed their hearts and minds to Jesus. He did a few miracles so that they were not without a witness.

"Amazed at their lack of faith" (v. 6) – It is worthy to note that God can be amazed by what we do. In this case, one would not want to amaze God with a lack of faith. But Jesus was truly amazed. After all He had said and done, His own hometown people rejected Him. Conversely, we see in Scripture where God can also be amazed by great faith (reference Matthew 8:5-13 about the Roman Centurion and Matthew 15:21-28 about the Canaanite woman).

The Book of Mark (Volume One)

 Insight Bible Commentary Series

V. Jesus Extends His Ministry Through His Disciples (Mark 6:6b-6:56)

At this time, Jesus begins to use His special disciples - the twelve chosen as Apostles - to extend His own ministry. He sends them out two-by-two to proclaim the message of His ministry (Mark 1:14-15). He gave them authority to heal people and cast out demons in His name. As King Herod hears about the miracles, he fears a prophet He had murdered (John the Baptist) had risen from the dead. A sidebar story explains how this happened.

As the disciples return to Jesus, He continues to teach them and mold their faith. He performs an amazing public miracle by turning a few loaves of bread into food for thousands. He walks on water to meet the disciples in their boat, encouraging them not to be afraid. Yet the disciples still did not understand the power of Jesus pointed to His divine nature.

A. Jesus sends out the twelve to preach, heal, and cast out demons (Mark 6:6b-13).

> *6 ... Then Jesus went around teaching from village to village. 7 Calling the Twelve to him, he began to send them out two by two and gave them authority over impure spirits. 8 These were his*

 Insight Bible Commentary Series

instructions: "Take nothing for the journey except a staff—no bread, no bag, no money in your belts. ⁹ Wear sandals but not an extra shirt. ¹⁰ Whenever you enter a house, stay there until you leave that town. ¹¹ And if any place will not welcome you or listen to you, leave that place and shake the dust off your feet as a testimony against them." ¹² They went out and preached that people should repent. ¹³ They drove out many demons and anointed many sick people with oil and healed them. (Mark 6:6b-13, NIV®)

Parallel passages: Matthew 10:1-15, Luke 9:1-6

Mark 6:6b-7: Jesus multiplies His ministry as He Himself teaches from town to town and also sends the Twelve out to preach the good news to towns in the area. Having mentored them personally, Jesus sends them out to really learn what they have been taught. It is through doing that we really learn life lessons. Bible study is necessary but incomplete until one applies the lessons in daily living – then we see that God's word is really true, that God is really faithful and wise, and that walking by faith is indeed the good life.

Mark 6:8-9: The disciples were told to go on a mission without the usual provisions one would need on any journey: no food, no bag for extra clothes, and no money. They would be forced to trust in God for the provisions they needed. He did allow them a staff – a long walking stick for the rocky terrain. It was also used to fight off wild animals.

Mark 6:10: As they entered a town and found someone hospitable enough to take in a stranger, they were instructed to stay there the whole time they preached in that town. This would bring great blessing to that household and – provide a witness to the town of God's care and concern for people.

Mark 6:11: *"Shake the dust off your feet"* – If the people in a town would not hear their message nor welcome the strangers, the disciples were to leave. They were not to force the good news on people who refused to hear. This is a lesson for us today in how to share the good news of God's grace with people we encounter. Yet the outright rejection of God's messengers came with a warning. The symbolic act of shaking the dust off their feet was enjoined upon Jews who passed through a Gentile (non-Jewish) town. For the Jews, this act was to rid themselves of any pagan influence they encountered.[24] As the disciples did this to the Jewish towns, they pronounced a warning from God that the Jews were acting like pagans and would be treated as such by God (unless, of course, they repented of their unbelief).

---

[24] Walvoord, John F. and Zuck, Roy B. *The Bible Knowledge Commentary: New Testament.* Victor Books: USA. Copyright 1983. p. 128.

Mark 6:12-13: The disciples declared Jesus message to *"repent and believe the good news" (Mark 1:15, NIV®)* of the kingdom of God. The word *"repent"* is from the Greek word "metanoeo," meaning to have a change of heart, to think differently than before. One's self-centered life must change to a God-centered life. While the good works follow such a change of heart, it is not good works that save (Ephesians 2:8-9). One must turn away from self and toward God through His Son, Jesus, who is the Messiah or Christ - our Savior.

Working under Jesus' authority (Mark 6:7), they were able to drive out demons and heal the sick.

"Anointed many sick people with oil" (v. 13) – In the desert climate, oil had many uses in protecting the skin and healing wounds. Anointing with oil was often done for such medicinal purposes. It was also used for various symbolic acts: consecration of priests (Exodus 29:1,7), consecration of the altar (Exodus 29:36), consecration of the Tabernacle and everything in it (Exodus 30:25-27), identification of a new king chosen by God (1 Samuel 10:1; 16:12-13; 1 Kings 1:39; 19:15), identification of a new prophet chosen by God (1 Kings 19:16). The title for Jesus "Messiah" quite literally means the "anointed one."

Sending His disciples out in His authority, he gave them instructions to anoint many sick people with oil to heal them. While the oil certainly helped, it did not heal them – God healed them. But this act would confirm the message of the disciples was from God and point them to His Messiah, Jesus. So the oil was both medicinal and symbolic in nature.

B. King Herod fears the power of John the Baptist in Jesus (Mark 6:14-29).

This passage juxtaposes two very different men - one godly and the other wicked:

John the Baptist	King Herod
John the Baptist was the last of the Old Testament prophets. His coming was predicted by Isaiah: *A voice of one calling: "In the wilderness prepare the way for the Lord; make straight in the desert a highway for our God. (Isaiah 40:3, NIV®).* John's ministry was to plough the rough ground in the hearts of the Jewish people to prepare them for the imminent coming of Messiah (Jesus). As a prophet, he clearly pointed out the sins of the people, urging them to repent and turn to God for forgiveness and reconciliation (Matthew 3:7-12). In fact, his message was very similar to the message of Jesus: *"Repent, for the kingdom of heaven is near."* (Matthew 3:2, NIV®)	There were several kings named Herod described in the Bible. Herod the Great (37 - 4 B.C.) was a builder during his reign, completing several significant structures including the rebuilding of the Temple and His palace. However the term "great" could also be used to describe his cruelty and evil bent. He ordered all male children two years old and younger to be murdered in his quest to kill Jesus. Herod the Great was the father of Herod Antipas (4 B.C. - 39 A.D.) who was the Tetrarch of Galilee and Perea.[25] Herod Antipas is the Herod that is described in this passage. It appears that he learned selfishness, pride, and cruelty from his father. Interestingly, this passage explains that Herod Antipas was actually afraid of John because he knew John was a righteous man of God (v. 20).

---

[25] *Ibid. p. 203.*

> *14 King Herod heard about this, for Jesus' name had become well known. Some were saying, "John the Baptist has been raised from the dead, and that is why miraculous powers are at work in him." 15 Others said, "He is Elijah." And still others claimed, "He is a prophet, like one of the prophets of long ago." 16 But when Herod heard this, he said, "John, whom I beheaded, has been raised from the dead!" (Mark 6:14-16, NIV®)*

Parallel passage: Matthew 14:1-2

Mark 6:14-16: Herod feared the miraculous works of Jesus because he thought that it was really John the Baptist raised from the dead. The guilt of his murder was still weighing heavily on Herod. Interestingly, there are no recorded miracles by John the Baptist nor are there any references to him driving out demons. Yet the people knew with certainty that John the Baptist was a prophet of God by the life he lived and the word of God that he spoke.

"Others said, 'He is Elijah.'" (v. 15) - There is a prophecy in the book of Malachi concerning the coming of Messiah (Christ):

> *5 "See, I will send you the prophet Elijah before that great and dreadful day of the LORD comes. 6 He will turn the hearts of the fathers to their*

 Insight Bible Commentary Series

children, and the hearts of the children to their fathers; or else I will come and strike the land with a curse." (Malachi 4:5-6, NIV®)

In the prophetic timeline, God would first send the prophet Elijah ahead of the Messiah. For this reason, some people reasoned that John the Baptist was perhaps Elijah raised from the dead. Jesus Himself confirmed that John the Baptist was fulfilling this prophecy:

11 I tell you the truth: Among those born of women there has not risen anyone greater than John the Baptist; yet he who is least in the kingdom of heaven is greater than he. 12 From the days of John the Baptist until now, the kingdom of heaven has been forcefully advancing, and forceful men lay hold of it. 13 For all the Prophets and the Law prophesied until John. 14 And if you are willing to accept it, he is the Elijah who was to come. 15 He who has ears, let him hear. (Matthew 11:11-14, NIV®)

Note that Jesus explained that John was not the resurrected Elijah. John was born of a woman (v. 11) - his mother was Elizabeth (Luke 1:13), a relative of Mary (Luke 1:36). So John was also a cousin of Jesus. He fulfilled the role of "the Elijah" (Matthew 11:14, NIV®) but he was not literally Elijah raised from the dead.

> *[17] For Herod himself had given orders to have John arrested, and he had him bound and put in prison. He did this because of Herodias, his brother Philip's wife, whom he had married. [18] For John had been saying to Herod, "It is not lawful for you to have your brother's wife." [19] So Herodias nursed a grudge against John and wanted to kill him. But she was not able to, [20] because Herod feared John and protected him, knowing him to be a righteous and holy man. When Herod heard John, he was greatly puzzled; yet he liked to listen to him. (Mark 6:17-20, NIV®)*

Parallel passages: Matthew 14:3-5

Mark 6:17-18: It is a dangerous thing to criticize even a good king, much less an evil one like Herod. Yet John was fulfilling his ministry as God's prophet. He spoke the same way to common people, Roman soldiers, and religious leaders. He replaced his fear with faith in God and in God's call on his life. What is your response to a bold witness for the LORD Jesus? Will you hang back in fear of being criticized, mocked, or physically endangered? Or will you walk by faith with confidence in God and His call on your life?

Mark 6:19: "So Herodias nursed a grudge against John and wanted to kill him. But she was not able to, because Herod feared John" (v. 19-20a) – Herodias was actually the wife of Herod's brother, Philip. She was offended that John the Baptist

would call her a sinner because of her adulterous marriage to Herod. She "nursed a grudge" – meaning she kept thinking about what John did and how much she hated him for it. When you have been offended by something that someone says to you, you need to take two specific actions:

i. Consider carefully the criticism. Is there any truth in what was said – even partially true? The hurtful words may have been intended only to strike out at you. Then again, there may be some underlying issue that you need to recognize. If so, you should repent and seek forgiveness from both God and the person you offended.

ii. For the offense you experienced, take responsibility for going to that person privately to work things out (Matthew 18:15). Herodias refused to do so and kept agonizing over the hurt. The process of forgiveness is intended to help you get over such offenses so you can reconcile with others. When you refuse to go through the process, a grudge remains and grows stronger.

Herodias had a grudge so strong she really wanted to kill John. She was prevented by Herod who was alternately afraid and intrigued as well as angry with John. In a moment, the story of Herodias' vengeance unfolds.

Mark 6:20: Herod placed John in prison (v. 17) when John the Baptist named Herod's sin of adultery (v. 18) and "all the other evil things he had done" (Luke 3:19, NIV®). Herod did this, not because of his own anger or indignation, but because of his wife's wrath (v.17). Like Adam, Herod allowed his wife to lead him astray.[26] Herod "feared John," "protected him," and knew "to be a righteous and holy man" (v. 20). He even "liked to listen to him" (v. 20). In spite of Herod's regard for John's righteousness, he locked him up to please his wife. Each one of us must battle this temptation to please others before pleasing God. Jesus made it clear: "Seek first His kingdom and His righteousness" (Matthew 6:33, NIV®). Do this, and the LORD will provide for your needs.

"He was greatly puzzled" (v. 20) - The word of God spoken through John the Baptist was curious to Herod. He did not grasp the meaning of much of what John preached because Herod was still self-centered, refusing God the "throne" of his own life. Yet "He liked to listen to him" (v. 20) anyway. The word of God is good for the soul and can be attractive even for those who are far

---

[26] *Genesis 3:6.*

from God. To be effective, though, the hearing of God's word must be accompanied by a heart open to obedience.

> ^{21} *Finally the opportune time came. On his birthday Herod gave a banquet for his high officials and military commanders and the leading men of Galilee.* ^{22} *When the daughter of Herodias came in and danced, she pleased Herod and his dinner guests. The king said to the girl, "Ask me for anything you want, and I'll give it to you."* ^{23} *And he promised her with an oath, "Whatever you ask I will give you, up to half my kingdom."* (Mark 6:21-23, NIV®)

Parallel passages: Matthew 14:6-7

Mark 6:21: It was an opportune time, but not for John the Baptist. Herod's pride is revealed as he gave himself a birthday party with the officials of his court as well as leading people from the community. Little did he know that his pride would trap him that very night.

Mark 6:22: The daughter of Herodias is not named in the Bible. The Jewish historian, Josephus, writes that her name was Salome.[27] She danced in a way that was very pleasing to Herod and his guests. Based on Herod's adulteress ways (ref. Mark 6:17-20), it is assumed that Salome's dance was provocative and

---

[27] *Josephus.* Jewish Antiquities. *Book XVIII, Chapter 5, 4.*

sensual. Her dancing pleased Herod so much that he made her a spectacular offer – anything she wanted, up to half his kingdom.

Mark 6:23: No doubt Herod and the others had too much to drink. In a sober state, it is doubtful Herod would have made such an offer. That is the danger in alcohol consumption. In moderation, it cheers the heart (Judges 9:13; Eccl. 2:3). But at some point it becomes too much and one loses control. The Bible makes it clear that drunkenness is a sin (Romans 13:13; Gal. 5:21; Eph. 5:18; 1 Tim. 3:3; Titus 1:7; 1 Pet. 4:3). Herod's loss of self-control cost him dearly. He even repeated the offer with an oath. Now the trap was set. Herod would be unable to break his oath because of all the officials and dignitaries he had invited to his own birthday party.

> *[24] She went out and said to her mother, "What shall I ask for?" "The head of John the Baptist," she answered. [25] At once the girl hurried in to the king with the request: "I want you to give me right now the head of John the Baptist on a platter." [26] The king was greatly distressed, but because of his oaths and his dinner guests, he did not want to refuse her. [27] So he immediately sent an executioner with orders to bring John's head. The man went, beheaded John in the prison, [28] and brought back his head on a platter. He presented it to the girl, and she gave it to her mother. [29] On hearing of this, John's disciples*

 Insight Bible Commentary Series

came and took his body and laid it in a tomb. (Mark 6:24-29, NIV®)

Parallel passages: Matthew 14:8-12

Mark 6:24-25: When Salome told her mother what she had been promised, Herodias seized the opportunity to have John the Baptist killed. Her grudge overcame any sense of morality or decency or even guilt. She asked for John to be executed immediately. Salome apparently had no problem honoring her mother's request. She *"hurried in to the king with the request" (v. 25)* Herodias must have raised Salome with the same disregard for the value of human life. *"I want you to give me right now the head of John the Baptist on a platter." (v25)* Not only did she want John executed but wanted him humiliated with his severed head paraded around the banquet hall.

Mark 6:26-29: King Herod was *"greatly distressed" (v. 26)* indicating he was truly grieved at the request to kill John the Baptist. Yet, again, he was more concerned about his reputation and pleasing his wife (and her daughter) than pleasing God. He had made an oath before his court officials and leading members of the community. So Herod ordered John's execution (v. 27). His head was placed on a platter and brought to Salome in front of the dinner guests. Salome then took John's head to her mother

(v. 28). What a frightful thing to witness at a dinner party! Herod and most of the guests had had too much to drink. One wonders what thoughts they had about this matter in the morning when the alcohol haze had cleared. But what is done is done. John the Baptist was dead and his grieving disciples gave him a proper burial (v. 29).

C. Jesus feeds five thousand with five loaves of bread and two fish (Mark 6:30-44).

> *30 The apostles gathered around Jesus and reported to him all they had done and taught. 31 Then, because so many people were coming and going that they did not even have a chance to eat, he said to them, "Come with me by yourselves to a quiet place and get some rest." 32 So they went away by themselves in a boat to a solitary place. 33 But many who saw them leaving recognized them and ran on foot from all the towns and got there ahead of them. 34 When Jesus landed and saw a large crowd, he had compassion on them, because they were like sheep without a shepherd. So he began teaching them many things. 35 By this time it was late in the day, so his disciples came to him. "This is a remote place," they said, "and it's already very late. 36 Send the people away so that they can go to the surrounding countryside and villages and buy themselves something to eat." 37 But he answered, "You give them something to eat." They said to him, "That would take more than half a year's wages! Are we to go and spend that much on bread and give it to them to eat?" 38*

 Insight Bible Commentary Series

"How many loaves do you have?" he asked. "Go and see." When they found out, they said, "Five—and two fish." ^{39} Then Jesus directed them to have all the people sit down in groups on the green grass. ^{40} So they sat down in groups of hundreds and fifties. ^{41} Taking the five loaves and the two fish and looking up to heaven, he gave thanks and broke the loaves. Then he gave them to his disciples to distribute to the people. He also divided the two fish among them all. ^{42} They all ate and were satisfied, ^{43} and the disciples picked up twelve basketfuls of broken pieces of bread and fish. ^{44} The number of the men who had eaten was five thousand. (Mark 6:30-44, NIV®)

Parallel passage: Matthew 14:13-21, Luke 9:10-17, John 6:1-13

Perhaps one of the more familiar stories in the Bible is this one regarding Jesus feeding five thousand men with a few loaves of bread and some fish. After so much ministry work to the villages surrounding Nazareth, the apostles were tired and hungry. Jesus took them across the Sea of Galilee to a private place where they could relax and debrief. Instead a crowd of people went ahead of them and met the boat as it arrived. Jesus taught them during the day and by evening, it was too late to send them away to get food. This set up the great miracle of feeding so many with so little.

Mark 6:30: The twelve apostles were sent out from Nazareth to preach and minister to the people in the surrounding villages (Mark 6:6-7). After this ministry work, they *"gathered around Jesus"* to talk about all that had transpired: preaching the good news of the kingdom (Mark 6:12), driving out demons and healing the sick (Mark 6:13). Matthew notes the apostles wanted to share with Jesus *"all they had done and taught."* The amazing miracles may have given the apostles the idea that special power had been conveyed to them. The miracle of feeding the five thousand would serve to correct this potential issue of pride.

Mark 6:31-32: The miracle-working ministry of Jesus' apostles stirred up the people. They were *"coming and going" (v. 31)* in the place where the apostles were trying to debrief with Jesus. Jesus recognized their need for rest and food so He encouraged them to go with Him to a private place across the Sea of Galilee. All ministry work, even working miracles, will deplete your physical, emotional, mental, and spiritual resources. No one can get around the need for sleep and refreshment – especially those involved in ministry work.

Mark 6:33-34: A great crowd of people looked for Jesus. They had a clear agenda: Jesus had miraculously healed the sick and they wanted to see for themselves (John 6:2). Ulterior motives or not, Jesus *"had compassion on them, because they were like*

 Insight Bible Commentary Series

sheep without a shepherd." (Mark 6:34a, NIV®) Sheep have a reputation in the animal kingdom of being quite dense. Certainly they have an instinctual habit of flocking together. Rather than thinking for themselves and acting independently, they follow one after the other when anything happens. So this comparison is not complementary at all. Keep in mind that this was a group of *regular* people – you and I are just as surely included in their number as if we had been there in person. What is the solution to being helpless like sheep? Jesus *"... began teaching them many things." (Mark 6:34b, NIV®)*

Mark 6:35-38: Lest anyone get the false impression that this miracle represents an act of social justice in feeding the hungry, this passage should settle the matter. The disciples recognized that the people were hungry and needed food. Their first thought was to simply send them away to get food for themselves. By their comment we glean that there were towns nearby where they could find food and drink. Certainly social justice was not on their minds.

Jesus gave them a curt but amazing response: *"You give them something to eat." (Mark 6:37, NIV®)* The disciples had very little compared to the vast crowd of people listening to Jesus. When asked how many loaves they had, the disciples replied, *"Five—and two fish."* (Mark 6:38, NIV®) They knew this was an insignificant amount and so did Jesus. And they pointed out to Jesus that it would take eight months wages to pay for enough food for this crowd. It is not suggested here that the disciples carried around that much money, simply a point of fact.

So why did Jesus tell them to do what He knew was impossible for them to do on their own? He wanted them to realize for themselves the impossibility of providing for the needs of so many. His point is that *"With man this is impossible, but with God all things are possible."* (Matthew 19:26, NIV®) Our provision in time and for eternity is assured through God alone. No matter how great the need, God is greater.

Mark 6:39-44: Jesus had the disciples get the people organized into groups from 50-100 to ensure an orderly distribution of the food He was about to provide. After giving thanks, Jesus began dividing the fish and bread among the disciples to give to the people. Imagine the surprise on the disciples faces as the few loaves of bread and fish kept multiplying so that the thousands of people could be fed.

The massive group of people received no small portion to eat. Verse 42 says that *"all ate and were satisfied."* (NIV®) The word translated *"satisfied"* is from the Greek word, "chortazo,"

 Insight Bible Commentary Series

which means to feed to the point of gorging. The people received a feast of bread and fish from the LORD Jesus. He not only met the hunger need but abundantly supplied that need. And there was no shortage of food – the disciples picked up a dozen basketfuls of fish and bread (v. 43), all originating from five loaves and two fish. The lesson is obvious. God who created all things can provide completely and abundantly more for all our needs. And He has promised to meet all our needs when we trust and follow Him (Matthew 6:33).

Note that the text says five thousand men were fed (v. 44). In this culture, only the men would have been counted. In reality, counting women and children who would surely not have been denied food to eat, the number of people fed could have easily been 15-20 thousand. But even if only five thousand were fed, it was still an astonishing miracle that pointed everyone who saw it to the divine hand of God. He was, and is, Jehovah-Jireh – the LORD will provide (Genesis 22:14).

D. Jesus walks on water (Mark 6:45-52).

> [45] Immediately Jesus made his disciples get into the boat and go on ahead of him to Bethsaida, while he dismissed the crowd. [46] After leaving them, he went up on a mountainside to pray. [47] Later that night, the boat was in the middle of the lake, and he was alone on land. [48] He saw the disciples straining at the oars, because the wind was against them. Shortly before dawn he went out to them, walking on the lake. He was about to pass by them, [49] but when they saw him walking on the lake, they thought he was a ghost. They cried out, [50] because they all saw him and were terrified. Immediately he spoke to them and said, "Take courage! It is I. Don't be afraid." [51] Then he climbed into the boat with them, and the wind died down. They were completely amazed, [52] for they had not understood about the loaves; their hearts were hardened. (Mark 6:45-52, NIV®)

Parallel passage: Matthew 14:22-33, John 6:16-21

After the astonishing miracle of feeding five thousand, Jesus performs an amazing miracle by walking on water. He sent the disciples on ahead of Him to Bethsaida while He dismissed the crowd and spent time alone in prayer. As the disciples struggled in a boat during a storm, Jesus almost casually starts to walk by them on the water. But He reassures them and puts an end to the storm they face when He enters the boat with them.

 Insight Bible Commentary Series

This passage is filled with powerful messages and symbolism that should not be missed.

Mark 6:45-46: No sooner had Jesus completed the astonishing miracle of feeding the five thousand than He sent His disciples *"Immediately" (v.45)* on ahead to the next ministry location: Bethsaida. Bethsaida means *House of Fish*, a common description for towns along the shore of the Sea of Galilee where fishing was an important component of the local economy. From Mark 6:53 we conclude that this Bethsaida was on the northeast end of the sea in the land of Gennesaret. So Jesus sent this band of mostly fishermen to the House of Fish to continue their training in how to fish for people.

Why, after leading the disciples away to a quiet place for rest (Mark 6:30), did Jesus send them back across the lake? It is not obvious in Mark's account. But in the gospel of John, we see that the people wanted to make Jesus their king by force (John 6:15). This was not God's plan for Jesus in His first appearance on Earth. He was to be a Savior not a King. There was to be no crown without the cross. This is why Jesus sent His disciples ahead and retreated to the mountain for solitude.

Note that Jesus *"made His disciples get into the boat." (v.45)* They must have been excited that Jesus was to be crowned King by the crowd and confused that He refused the offer. So Jesus had to insist that they go back.

It was also a long day of ministry. So Jesus went up to a secluded spot on the mountainside to pray (v. 46). Jesus was unquestionably very tired. But prayer provided Jesus with the strength and direction He needed for ministry. There is a direct correlation between the quantity of ministry work and the need for prayer. One cannot ignore the necessity and power of prayer for doing God's work. As someone once said, *"If you are too busy to pray, then you are too busy NOT to pray!"*

Mark 6:47-50: The disciples had a hard time crossing the lake in a boat. It was dark, in the fourth watch of the day (v. 48) which is between 3am and 6am.[28] The wind was pushing at them making their rowing unproductive. What a classic picture this is of how impossible it is to complete God's work without God in the middle of it all. Jesus observed their difficulties and eventually started walking across the lake.

At this point the disciples were terrified. They were tired, confused, perhaps let down from the possibility of Jesus

---

[28] *The NIV® translates* tetarthn fulakhn *as* shortly before dawn. *The Greek is literally translated* fourth watch. *The night watch was broken down into four watches: first watch 6pm-9pm, second watch 9pm-12am, third watch 12am-3am, and the fourth watch 3am-6am.*

 Insight Bible Commentary Series

becoming the King. The dark, stormy night was creepy. To make matters worse, in the distance, they saw a ghost (v.49). At least the circumstances led them to think such a thing. Some of the disciples even began to scream.

Obviously the disciples had not made the connection between Jesus and His innate divinity and heavenly power. While they were doing what He asked them to do, they were still without faith and trust in Him. So Jesus gave them this test to see how they would react. The crisis of enduring the storm alone had raised their fear. At this point, Jesus showed up.

Mark 6:50-52: In the darkest time, the disciples had no courage. Jesus spoke just a few words with significant impact (v. 50):

- *"Take courage!"* – The courage the disciples needed was only available from the Creator of the Universe.

- *"It is I."* – No situation is truly hopeless in the presence of Jesus.

- *"Don't be afraid."* – Fear is natural. But you can belay your fears and put them aside when Jesus is with you.

One might attribute some courage to Peter. In Matthew's account, Peter called out to Jesus, *"Lord, if it's you ... tell me to come to you on the water." (Matthew 14:28, NIV®)* Yet his courage failed as he walked on the water toward Jesus. The wind was strong and the night was still dark. Peter's small bit of courage gave way to fear and he began to sink. True courage is a reflection of faith. The fear may be real but courage requires that you move forward in spite of your fear. Faith enables you move in the direction of Jesus no matter how dire the circumstances.

Jesus further drove home the point He was making with the disciples when He climbed into the boat. He stepped over the edge and immediately the wind died down. Jesus, Creator of all things, had no trouble at all calming the storm. Mark notes the amazement of the disciples (v. 51) and the fact that they had still not made the important faith connection about Jesus' divinity and power (v. 52). In spite of the miracle of feeding so many with just a few loaves of bread, their faith was still emerging.

In the midst of difficult circumstances, it is easy for us to give way to fear. Faith demands that when we are afraid, we should turn to the LORD and trust in Him (Psalm 56:3-4). This is not a one-time, fix-it-all event. When we fear, we trust and keep on trusting. When we feel fear again, we trust and keep on trusting. There is no difficult to great for the LORD. There is no circumstance beyond the help of the One who spoke the universe into existence.

E. Jesus heals all that touch Him in the land of Gennesaret (Mark 6:53-56)

> ⁵³ *When they had crossed over, they landed at Gennesaret and anchored there.* ⁵⁴ *As soon as they got out of the boat, people recognized Jesus.* ⁵⁵ *They ran throughout that whole region and carried the sick on mats to wherever they heard he was.* ⁵⁶ *And wherever he went—into villages, towns or countryside—they placed the sick in the marketplaces. They begged him to let them touch even the edge of his cloak, and all who touched it were healed. (Mark 6:53-56, NIV®)*

As Jesus and the disciples landed on the other side of the lake, the people saw Jesus and rushed to get their sick to Him. All who were brought to Jesus were healed of their physical ailments. The question remains on how many were healed of their spiritual ailment?

Mark 6:53-54: Crossing over to the west side of the lake, Jesus and the disciples arrived in the land of Gennesaret. While they were directed to the town of Bethsaida (Mark 6:45), the reference here is to an area of very fertile land (Gennesaret means the *garden of the prince*) in which Bethsaida was located. The people of this area knew very well about Jesus' power and reputation. The word "recognized" translates "epiginosko" meaning to know based on prior knowledge and being fully acquainted with the subject.

Mark 6:55:56: The excitement of the people was not about the wonderful truths from God that Jesus wanted to share. Rather they wanted to see Jesus heal people – whether it was purely compassion or also the entertainment value is not clear. Nevertheless, they zealously found the sick among them and brought them to Jesus.

The people *"begged him to let them touch even the edge of his cloak." (v. 56)* One thing is clear: they truly believed that Jesus had the power to heal instantly any sickness. Jesus provided healing for *"all who touched it."* Not every sick person in the area was healed; only those who were brought to Jesus. Certainly this is a key learning for us today. Ultimate healing, the forgiveness of sins and a regenerated spirit, can only come from Jesus. It is up to believers to bring non-believers to Jesus for salvation.

One must be sure to differentiate the physical healing from the spiritual healing of Jesus. The miracles of healing performed by Jesus were for the purpose of authenticating His message of the kingdom of God. As He began His ministry, Jesus proclaimed, *"The kingdom of God has come near. Repent*

 Insight Bible Commentary Series

and believe the good news!" (Mark 1:15, NIV®) Some teach that salvation always includes physical healing, citing *"by his wounds we are healed." (Isaiah 53:5, NIV®)* To be sure, Jesus has the power to heal anything for anyone at any time, including today. But spiritual healing is clearly the context of the passage in Isaiah 53:4-6 since Jesus was crucified for *"transgressions"* and *"iniquities,"* a punishment on Him that *"brought us peace"* with God. In the final analysis, physical healing will surely occur at the resurrection where our heavenly bodies will never grow old or get sick again (Revelation 21:4). In this life, however, sickness is the sad reality of living in a sin-cursed world. Jesus never promised to take away all our troubles but that He would be with us through every moment we live (Matthew 28:20; John 6:33).

END OF VOLUME ONE

The Book of Mark (Volume One)

 Insight Bible Commentary Series

Complete Outline of Mark

The commentary on Mark is being published in multiple volumes. Volume one covers chapters 1-6. Below you will find a detailed outline of the entire Insight Bible Commentary on Mark.

Volume 1

1. **Overview of the Gospel of Mark (Mark 1:1).**

    A. Purpose
    B. Authorship
    C. Outline and Chronology
    D. Contribution

2. **Jesus Prepares For His Earthly Ministry (Mark 1:2-13).**

    A. Jesus is announced by John the Baptist (Mark 1:2-8).
    B. Jesus is identified by God as His beloved Son (Mark 1:9-11).
    C. Jesus overcomes temptation in the wilderness (Mark 1:12-13).
    D. Conclusion of section 2.

 Insight Bible Commentary Series

3. **Jesus Begins His Earthly Ministry in Galilee (Mark 1:14-3:35).**

   A. In Capernaum (Mark 1:14-34).

      (1) Jesus proclaims the message of His ministry (Mark 1:14-15).
      (2) Jesus calls His first disciples (Mark 1:16-20).
      (3) Jesus commands authority over demons (Mark 1:21-28).
      (4) Jesus commands power over sickness (Mark 1:29-31).
      (5) Jesus commands power over all who are sick (Mark 1:32-34).
      (6) Conclusion of Section A.

   B. Traveling Through Galilee (Mark 1:35-2:12).

      (1) Jesus proclaims the purpose of His ministry (Mark 1:35-39).
      (2) Jesus heals a leper (Mark 1:40-45).
      (3) Jesus forgives the sins of a lame man (Mark 2:1-12).

   C. Encountering Questions (Mark 2:13-3:6).

      (1) Jesus ministers to publicans and sinners (Mark 2:13-17).
      (2) Jesus delineates new ways for the new life He offers (Mark 2:18-22).
      (3) Jesus defies the Sabbath traditions of men (Mark 2:23-28).
      (4) Pharisees begin their plot to kill Jesus (Mark 3:1-6).

D. Organizing the Disciples (Mark 3:7-35).

  (1) Jesus teaches multitudes from Israel and the surrounding nations (Mark 3:7-12).
  (2) Jesus calls out His twelve disciples (Mark 3:13-19).
  (3) Scribes accuse Jesus of being demon-possessed (Mark 3:20-30).
  (4) Jesus shares a close relationship with those who do God's will (Mark 3:31-35).

4. **Jesus prepares His disciples (Mark 4:1-6:6).**

  A. Jesus teaches His disciples through parables (Mark 4:1-34).

   (1) Parable of the sower (Mark 4:1-9).
   (2) Jesus explains His use of parables (Mark 4:10-12).
   (3) Jesus explains the parable of the sower (Mark 4:13-20).
   (4) Jesus announces the keys to understanding the kingdom of God (Mark 4:21-25).
   (5) Parable of the growing seed (Mark 4:26-29).
   (6) Parable of the mustard seed (Mark 4:30-32).
   (7) Jesus uses parables for the people but explains all to His disciples (Mark 4:33-34).

 Insight Bible Commentary Series

    B.   Jesus teaches His disciples through miracles (Mark 4:35-6:6).

        (1)   Jesus calms the wind and the sea (Mark 4:35-41).
        (2)   Jesus drives out a legion of demons into a herd of pigs (Mark 5:1-20).
        (3)   Jesus heals the sick and raises the dead (Mark 5:21-43).
        (4)   Jesus heals only a few sick people in His hometown (Mark 6:1-6a).

5.   **Jesus Extends His Ministry Through His Disciples (Mark 6:6b-6:56).**

    A.   Jesus sends out the twelve to preach, heal, and cast out demons (Mark 6:6b-13).
    B.   King Herod fears the power of John the Baptist in Jesus (Mark 6:14-29).
    C.   Jesus feeds five thousand with five loaves of bread and two fish (Mark 6:30-44).
    D.   Jesus walks on water (Mark 6:45-52).
    E.   Jesus heals all that touch Him in the land of Gennesaret (Mark 6:53-56).

Volume 2

6. **Jesus encounters opposition to His ministry (Mark 7:1-8:30).**

   A. Criticism Over Tradition (Mark 7:1-23).

   (1) Criticism regarding ceremony (Mark 7:1-5).
   (2) Criticism regarding traditions of men (Mark 7:6-13).
   (3) Criticism regarding uncleanness (Mark 7:14-23).

   B. Demanding a Sign (Mark 7:24-8:12).

   (1) Jesus drives out a demon from a Gentile woman's daughter (Mark 7:24-30).
   (2) Jesus heals a deaf and dumb man in Galilee (Mark 7:31-37).
   (3) Jesus feeds four thousand with seven loaves of bread and a few fish (Mark 8:1-10).
   (4) The Pharisees demand a miraculous sign from Jesus (Mark 8:11-12).

   C. Countering Opposition With Truth (Mark 8:13-30).

   (1) Jesus warns the disciples of the teachings of the Pharisees (Mark 8:13-21).
   (2) Jesus heals a blind man in Galilee (Mark 8:22-26).
   (3) Peter declares that Jesus is the Christ (Mark 8:27-30).

7. **Jesus Moves His Ministry to Jerusalem (Mark 8:31-10:52).**

    A.   The cost of following Jesus (Mark 8:31-9:13).

        (1)   Jesus foretells His rejection and suffering in Jerusalem (Mark 8:31-33).
        (2)   Jesus pronounces the cost of following Him (Mark 8:34-38).
        (3)   Jesus is transfigured on a high mountain (Mark 9:1-13).

    B.   The demands of faith (Mark 9:14-10:12).

        (1)   Jesus drives out a demon that caused a boy to be deaf and dumb (Mark 9:14-29).
        (2)   Jesus foretells His death and resurrection (Mark 9:30-32).
        (3)   Jesus teaches greatness through humble service to others (Mark 9:33-37).
        (4)   Jesus warns against divisiveness among His disciples (Mark 9:38-41).
        (5)   Jesus warns of the terrible reality of Hell for sinners (Mark 9:42-48).
        (6)   Jesus exhorts His disciples to be at peace with one another (Mark 9:49-50).
        (7)   Jesus teaches about the sanctity of marriage (Mark 10:1-12).

C. Finding salvation (Mark 10:13-31).

    (1) Jesus receives and blesses little children (Mark 10:13-16).
    (2) Jesus teaches a rich, young ruler about eternal life (Mark 10:17-22).
    (3) Jesus explains salvation is from God not man (Mark 10:23-31).

D. Suffering and glory (Mark 10:32-52).

    (1) Jesus foretells His death and resurrection (Mark 10:32-34).
    (2) Jesus defines greatness (Mark 10:35-45).
    (3) Jesus heals the persistent blind man (Mark 10:46-52).

8. Jesus confronts Jerusalem with His authority (Mark 11:1-13:37).

A. Presentation of the King (Mark 11:1-26).

    (1) Jesus approaches Jerusalem as the King of Israel (Mark 11:1-11).
    (2) Jesus curses a barren fig tree (Mark 11:12-14).
    (3) Jesus cleanses the Temple (Mark 11:15-19).
    (4) Jesus commands His disciples to have faith in God (Mark 11:20-24).
    (5) Jesus stresses the need to forgive others (Mark 11:25-26).

 Insight Bible Commentary Series

    B.   Testing of the King (Mark 11:27-12:44).

        (1)   Religious leaders confront Jesus about His authority (Mark 11:27-33).
        (2)   Jesus tells the parable of the vineyard owner (Mark 12:1-12).
        (3)   Pharisees and Herodians test Jesus concerning taxes (Mark 12:13-17).
        (4)   Sadducees test Jesus concerning the resurrection (Mark 12:18-27).
        (5)   Jesus teaches a scribe about the greatest commandment (Mark 12:28-34).
        (6)   Jesus tests the scribes concerning the identity of the Christ (Mark 12:35-37).
        (7)   Jesus warns against the hypocrisy of the scribes (Mark 12:38-40).
        (8)   Jesus praises the gift of a poor widow (Mark 12:41-44).

Volume 3

    C.   Prophetic Discourse of the King on End-Time Events (Mark 13:1-37).

        (1)   A temporal versus eternal perspective (Mark 13:1-2).
        (2)   Increasing strife and persecution will require endurance (Mark 13:3-13).
        (3)   The great tribulation period (Mark 13:14-23).
        (4)   The second coming of Christ (Mark 13:24-27).
        (5)   Interpreting the signs of the times (Mark 13:28-31).

(6) The need to watch and pray (Mark 13:32-37).

9. **Jesus is Betrayed and Crucified (Mark 14:1-15:47).**

   A. Conspiracy against Jesus (Mark 14:1-42).

   (1) Religious leaders plot to kill Jesus (Mark 14:1-2).
   (2) Mary annoints Jesus for His burial (Mark 14:3-9).
   (3) Judas conspires with the chief priests to betray Jesus (Mark 14:10-11).
   (4) Jesus celebrates His last Passover meal with His disciples (Mark 14:12-21).
   (5) Jesus initiates the LORD's Supper (Mark 14:22-26).
   (6) Peter and the disciples promise to die for Jesus (Mark 14:27-31).
   (7) Jesus prays in Gethsemane (Mark 14:32-42).

   B. Arrest and Trial of Jesus (Mark 14:43-15:20).

   (1) Jesus is betrayed and arrested (Mark 14:43-52).
   (2) Jesus is beaten and accused by the Sanhedrin (Mark 14:53-65).
   (3) Peter denies he is a disciple of Jesus three times (Mark 14:66-72).
   (4) Pilate interrogates Jesus (Mark 15:1-5).
   (5) Pilate delivers Jesus over to be crucified (Mark 15:6-15).

 Insight Bible Commentary Series

        (6)   Roman soldiers mock Jesus as the King of the Jews (Mark 15:16-20).

    C.   Crucifixion of Jesus (Mark 15:21-47).

        (1)   Roman soldiers crucify Jesus (Mark 15:21-26).
        (2)   The crowd and religious leaders mock Jesus as He is crucified (Mark 15:27-32).
        (3)   Jesus dies for the sins of the whole world (Mark 15:33-41).
        (4)   Joseph of Arimathaea buries Jesus in a rock tomb (Mark 15:42-47).

10.   **Jesus is Vindicated By His Resurrection From the Dead (Mark 16:1-20).**

    A.   An angel announces the resurrection of Jesus (Mark 16:1-8).
    B.   The dispute over Mark 16:9-20 in manuscript evidence.
    C.   The resurrected Jesus appears first to a woman, Mary Magdalene (Mark 16:9-11).
    D.   The resurrected Jesus appears to two disciples on the Emmaus road (Mark 16:12-13).
    E.   The resurrected Jesus appears to the eleven disciples and commissions them to preach the gospel (Mark 16:14-18).
    F.   Jesus ascends to Heaven and the disciples carry out their commission (Mark 16:19-20).

The Book of Mark (Volume One)

 Insight Bible Commentary Series

About the Author

Randy Lariscy is an evangelist, Bible Teacher, and author of several books. As a bivocational minister, Randy was licensed at Roswell Street Baptist church and ordained at Noonday Baptist Church in Marietta, Georgia. Working in both business and ministry vocations has provided Randy with unique set of skills which he uses for God's glory and to further His kingdom.

His various roles in ministry have included:

- Evangelism Consultant
- Education Pastor
- Supply Preacher
- Radio Bible Teacher

He holds a Master of Arts in Pastoral Ministry from Trinity Theological Seminary and a Master of Divinity. He has been married for over 30 years to Mary, a registered nurse, and they have two adult children. They reside in Kennesaw, Georgia.

Quality resources with significant spiritual impact

On the web at www.WordTruthPress.com

Find more great resources from WordTruth Press:

	Portraits of Forgiveness *Finding the Inspiration and Courage to Forgive* Like an old, frayed blanket there are many loose threads in our relationships. Issues and conflict divide us from family, friends, and innumerable people we encounter throughout life. The process of forgiveness is necessary to restore and rebuild those relationships. In this book you will find great stories of how God works in the lives of people to bring about forgiveness and reconciliation - binding up the loose threads and making relationships even stronger than before.
 *Available now* *$9.95 USD*	

 *Coming soon!*	**The Evangelism Engine** *Build a Sustainable Evangelism Ministry in Your Church* Evangelism is a ministry of the church that usually runs hot or cold depending on the passion and energy of one person in the church. The Evangelism Engine enables churches to establish evangelism as a sustainable, long-term process. For pastors and ministry leaders.
 *Coming Soon!*	**Natural Evangelism** *Learn to Share the Love and Message of Christ* Natural Evangelism helps individual believers understand and embrace the call to be a disciple-making disciple. This practical training covers multiple approaches to sharing the good news of God's grace, techniques for visiting with people, and how to find prospects for the kingdom of God.

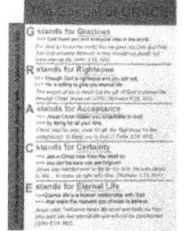

$9.95 USD
Qty 50

The Gospel of GRACE
Evangelism Tract (Qty 50)

This attractive 3x5 card presents the good news using the word GRACE as an acrostic. Each letter represents a different aspect of God's grace at work in salvation. Glossy, color front and black-and-white back.

$9.95 USD
Qty 50

The Ten Commandments
Evangelism Tract (Qty 50)

The Ten Commandments tract has an attractive design for displaying the "big ten" commands and it also provides a positive statement of each command. "You shall have no other Gods before Me" can also be stated as "Put God First!" Glossy, color front and black-and-white back.

Speedy Devotions
Volume One – Wise Choices

Available Now
$12.95 USD

Speedy Devotions is intended for people who think they have little time to study the Bible. The Bible can certainly be intimidating in its size and scope. Many find it hard to stay focused on long passages of Scripture. Yet the Bible is God's word for all people. And even a small amount of God's word can have a profound impact on your life.

The format of this devotional is simple. Each day you will encounter:

- **God's Word:** Only one or two Bible verses to consider.
- **Life Principle:** A short thought based God's word to help you understand the key teaching.
- **Life Change:** Space to reflect and record the life change you need to make.

The mission of WordTruth Press is to provide quality Bible-based resources with significant spiritual impact for individuals and churches. Education and evangelism are the main focus of WordTruth Press. Following the Great Commission of the LORD Jesus (Matthew 28:18-20), this organization provides Bible-based resources to evangelize the world, encourage and equip believers and churches for evangelism, and provide solid Bible teaching to build up the body of Christ.

A key strategy is to find low-cost channels for production and distribution to maximize the availability of our resources to people around the world. WordTruth Press also offers many free resources for churches and individuals available online at:

www.WordTruthPress.com

www.ingramcontent.com/pod-product-compliance
Lightning Source LLC
Chambersburg PA
CBHW022355040426
42450CB00005B/193